D0499066

Satisfying
the
Black Man
Sexually

Made Simple

By Dr. Rosie Milligan

Published by
Professional Business Consultants

Editing and Typesetting by Vivian Hudson
Photography by Roderick Solomon

ISBN 1-881524-04-3

Men Have Lost Their Jobs For It

Men Have Lost Their Lives For It

Men Have Left Their Wives For IT

Men Have Left School For It

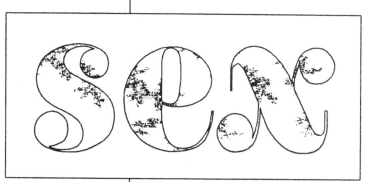

All For A Little Piece

Of Real Estate With

Grass Growing On It

This Book Will Teach

You How To Keep

Up The Lawn

Table of Contents

PLEASE NOTE...

The external reproductive organs of the Black man are the same as men of other ethnic groups. However, it has been said that his penis is larger. Some of the fears, hang-ups, likes and dislikes may blend in with men of other races. Therefore, you will find that some issues discussed are not the exclusive feelings of the Black man. All men have some things in common and there is no getting around it. Nevertheless, my main focus is the Black man because of the various social, psychological, and economical factors that have greatly impacted his life and, therefore, his sexuality.

Personal Acknowledgments

I am truly thankful to Barbara Lindsey of Lindsey and Associates for insisting that I write this book. She is a promoter and has been saying for years "Rosie, you have too much to say, not to say it. I would love to promote you as a speaker but you have got to get some products." Thank you Barbara for pushing me to excellence.

To Ruby Smith, who has said, "Girl I see greatness in you." Thank you for believing in me.

Barbara, Ruby and I have been friends since our high school days. Both of them never allowed me to quit. When I would stop, they would not accept it, they would say: "You have not quit, you are just resting."

To my friend and business partner, Mary Lee Crump, who has always made "such-a-to-do" out of everything that I have ever done. I thank you for being there for me, emotionally and financially.

I also want to acknowledge my loving children: Pamela Milligan, M.D., John Jr., and Cedric, my assistant business manager. They believe that if I didn't say it, it has no merit nor value.

To Mr. Jackie Roy and Mrs. Theresa Johnson of LeRoy, Alabama, thank you for encouragement, and for manufacturing an herbal product that improves male sexual potency. (STIF HERBAL TONIC)

I want to acknowledge my sisters and brothers who have considered me their mentor. Especially my sister Clara Hunter King, who has shared all of my woes throughout childhood and my adult life. Thanks Clara. Kenyaka Mamahi, my baby sister, who called everyday to see how far I was from the finishing line on the book. Now it's here.

To Armentria Johnson, my godmother who had all the answers to questions that I could not find during my research. She has certainly not been asleep for three scores. Love you.

Special thanks to all those men who participated in the survey. This book is a part of you! Whoops, here it is!

Biography

Dr. Rosie Milligan, registered nurse, health consultant, author and Ph.D. in business administration, has been an achiever most of her life. She has always been involved in a career or business in which she was helping other people accomplish what they want in life. Her motto, "Erase No--Step Over Can't and Move Forward with Life," has been a motivating influence to hundreds whom she has been mentor and role model.

The mother of three entrepreneurs, lectures nationally on male-female relations, human sexuality and mental and physical hygiene. Her book, *Satisfying the Black Woman Sexually Made Simple* has benefitted scores of Americans and received much acclaim.

Dr. Milligan has taught nursing education and was Director of Nursing for the College Allied Health Careers and for the Los Angeles Job Corps Center. She assisted in writing the competency-based Educational Curriculum for Geriatric Nursing for the National Job Corps and holds a life teaching credential for the State of California.

Foreword

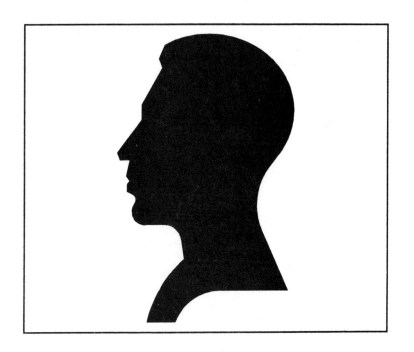

by Randall W. Maxey, M.D., Ph.D.

Foreword

This book addresses a difficult but pertinent subject matter that is long overdue. As an inner city practicing physician specializing in internal medicine, hypertension and kidney disease, each day I encounter the challenges of the sexuality of the Black male. As most people now know, Blacks in general, but Black males in particular, are affected by a higher incidence of many illnesses than are whites and generally with a greater severity.

Many of these disease entities have a direct or indirect influence on a male's ability to carry out sexual function. For the purpose of background, William Casey, M.D. states that the ability to have normal penile erections is dependent upon four factors: psychologic adequacy, intact innervation (nerve supply) of the penis, adequate blood flow to the penis and sufficient hormone levels.

Dr. Milligan astutely speaks to each of these issues in an easily readable, clear and understandable manner. She clearly presents material that outlines the physiologic mechanisms that are associated with the sexual act and physical responses of both sexes that lead to a satisfying relationship, but more important in a very sensitive and insightful way, she identifies and adds an expansion on what I think is the key area of relevance, that of the effect of Psychology, Socio Economic and Health on the sexuality of the Black male.

Psychologic adequacy is primary in the male sexual response. This, of course, has to be extremely affected by such things as self image and levels of stress. Dr. Milligan expounds on the residual effects on the psyche being raised in a nation where your ancestors were slaves and therefore not considered human. And living in a country which still has the vestiges of that same calculated system of human mind enslavement and denigration.

Admittedly, the laws have changed, but the system and thought process of racism and slavery and certainly economic entrapment of great masses of Black people are still firmly in place, along with their attendant negative effects.

In recent years, science and medicine have accepted the evidence as fact that there is a clear relationship between the psyche and physiologic function. This book effectively talks about how our history of Black male oppression may play an active role in Black male relationships with, not only Black and White women, but with other people in general--especially family.

The author suggests that society has inculcated both the Black man and society in general, into the mythical belief that he, the Black man, is a sexual animal or stud. When this normal, healthy man finds that he is "only" human, not super human in bed, it only adds another failure to his already heavy burden of feelings of inadequacy resulting from social and economic insecurity. This results in difficult sexual relations which negatively impacts all of his relationships with women. Dr. Milligan speaks of a self-fulfilling prophecy that can create either dysfunction in sexuality or, at the very least, vastly unsatisfactory male-female relationships.

The best part of this book, however, are recipes for enhancement or correction of relationships and sexual response. Dr. Milligan quotes a list of 101 ways to pamper your man, which ends with praying for and with him.

A key section deals with the effect on sexual ability of a number of diseases and their respective therapies. Most notably, the author speaks of how many Black men forego their anti-hypertensive medication for fear that their sexual ability will be decreased. Newer medications have overcome several of these problems which have previously resulted in impotence for many individuals.

This book covers a broad area where there previously existed a gap of reliable information. Of importance is not only the scientific and literary validation provided, but the historical perspective maintained throughout. It is a must read for all health professionals and any person of any color involved with life.

Randall W. Maxey, M.D., Ph.D.

Preface

Sexual double standards have placed full responsibility for the failure or success of sexual intercourse upon the man. Good sex is when a man and a woman take the time to explore each other fully and learn to work together for mutual gratification. However, often time the Black man finds himself in a position that makes him feel like he is a sexual performer because society has stigmatized him with myths regarding his sexuality. He has been labeled as "Mandingo," "Long John," and a sexual robot full of energy with everlasting endurance.

The Black man takes those myths into the bedroom with him. He needs constant validation that he is all that he is supposed to be. If the Black man does not receive this validation, he will continue to seek it from his woman or another woman.

I have surveyed and interviewed over one thousand men in the past two years and have found them to be eager to share their likes and dislikes about sex. Even after my lectures, I am often bombarded by men wanting to know more about sexual fulfillment, relationships and when my book *Satisfying The Black Man* would be published.

One gentleman called to tell me that he was ready for a divorce but he was going to wait until my book was

19

published in hopes that things would change after his wife read the book. I asked him had he read my book on *Satisfying The Black Woman Sexually Made Simple*. He replied no, because satisfying a woman sexually is a natural thing for a man to do.

The Black man takes pride in the fact that he has an asset that the White man cannot take from him: his large penis. I used to hear Black men joke about the "White man with the money and the Negro with the honey."

Since the Black man has been deprived both socially and economically, my intention is that he not also be deprived sexually. Sexual empowerment and enjoyment should be a basic right, since there is no law that prohibits the enjoyment of such for any man.

The Black woman will welcome this book because she has always had a strong desire to please her Black man. Nevertheless, she needs to understand that it is critical that Black men be examined and validated based on standards outside of the European value system and according to his own culture, experiences and opportunities made available to him. The Black man will ultimately benefit by developing a greater awareness and better understanding of his own sexuality.

The White woman will embrace this book because she wants to make sure she gains an edge on her competitor, the Black woman.   And lastly, The White man will finally satisfy his curiosity about the Black man's sexuality which he has pondered for more than 500 years.

Introduction

The Black man's sexuality is a subject that I have wanted to address for decades. However, I chose to address the Black woman's sexuality first, because most divorces and separations among Black families are initiated by the Black woman.

Based on my research, I have found that sexual chaos and bedroom turmoil are among the leading forces contributing to the high divorce rate in our society as a whole. Sex is not a cure, but it can soothe the pain. Sex has a profound effect on our lives and influences almost everything we do. It impacts how we rear our children, relate to the significant mate in our lives, and how we interact with our colleagues in the work place. Therefore, I believe it is high time that we address it head on with honesty and open mindedness.

When married couples enter the divorce court for a divorce decree, the divorce is granted based on irreconcilable differences. It would be interesting to hear responses if the judges required couples to explain their irreconcilable differences. If sex was not a taboo subject, I would guarantee you that many would say "I am sexually frustrated." This is best exemplified in an article written by Susan Jacoby in the December, 1991 issue of *New Woman Magazine* where a married woman shared her frustration as she states:

I would feel angry and deprived but I would never admit it had anything to do with sex. Instead, I would explode at him about something totally unrelated. I hated myself and I had a kind of contempt for him because he had not figured out what I wanted without my telling him. Finally, when I couldn't stand it anymore, I told him the truth, he walked out on me.

The lack of understanding regarding the Black man's sexuality and factors that impact the Black man's sexuality are causing serious problems within the Black community. The community as a whole is being jeopardized because of "Sexuality Confusion." My objective for dealing with the subject of the Black man's sexuality is to give credence to the fact that a problem does exist. And to provide a catalyst for open dialogue in hopes that Blacks will develop a greater sensitivity towards each other and the walls that have destroyed the Black family structure can be torn down so that healing, restoration and unification of the Black race can take hold again.

The purpose of this book is not to cast blame nor to point fingers at the Black male nor female, but to show how the Eurocentric belief and value systems forced upon us have lead up to this state of confusion and therefore separation. We must realize that the solution to our dilemma begins with understanding who we are as a people, how we got to this present state in the first place, and how we can work it out within ourselves by establishing our own value and belief systems and reclaiming our culture. We must realize that Blacks are unique and not Ebony European Clones. The Black experience is different, therefore our sexuality is different.

Knowing that sex is a dominating factor in our lives, that moving force that keeps us going, an obscure, paradoxical and biological necessity that dominates and impacts our lives in every way, I am compelled to research and address it wholeheartedly in hopes of bringing Black people out of darkness and confusion and into complete understanding and awareness of Black sexuality.

Chapter 1

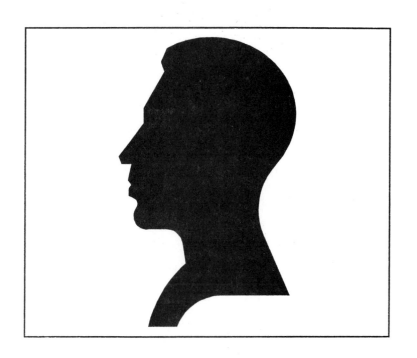

Overview of the Black Man's Sexuality

The lack of understanding regarding the Black man's sexuality and the factors that impact his sexuality are causing serious problems within the Black community. The entire Black community is being jeopardized because of "Sexuality Confusion." Haki R. Madhubuti in *Black Men Obsolete, Single, Dangerous?* had the following to say about sexuality:

Male and female sexuality has been suppressed by Christian thought. Sexual pleasure in the past has been condemned as a sin, and its suppression has aided men and women in developing new forms of perversion and neurosis. The emergence of rape, pornography and incest (Butler, 1979) is closely related to psycho-sexual problems. The most sought after experience by humans, after eating, is sex, and to continuously keep it in the closet will undoubtedly cause serious problems for future generations.

Sex is not everything in a nutshell, however, sex has an effect on everything we do. A couple needs much more than sex to bridge and sustain a well balanced healthy relationship. Sexual activities have a strong influence on the way one thinks and performs in all areas of activity.

William McQueen supports this point of view in *The X-Rated Sex Book*:

> Except for money, sex is the only factor in our civilized societies that people contemplate at the risk of causing harm to themselves, their families, or to the loss of their jobs, and all for a few short hours of pleasure and a few seconds of orgasmic thrills. It is the only factor that can cause a community wide, a city wide, or a national or international calamity. And just think, all it entails is a minimum of two people fucking each other by their own consent. But if you do it in a manner in which people say is wrong, they will destroy you! Sex, a dominating factor in our lives...that moving force that keeps us going, and most of us even admit it. Sex, that obscure and yet paradoxically, mundane, biological necessity that dominates us all in one way or another.

Ishakamus Barashango in *Afrikan Woman the Original Guardian Angel* made the following statement regarding sexuality:

> As evidenced, puritanical societies where sexual harmony is repressed tend to be more violent and aggressive. Now I am not citing this in a spirit of abject promiscuity or to emphasize mere biological gratification, but rather as a reaffirmation of ancient Afrikan High Culture societies' general attitudes toward and genuine concern for the achievement of a cosmic balance in human sexuality.

30

We must understand that cultural difference brings about sexual difference. The Black man is not an Ebony Caucasian clone. His experiences are different, therefore, his sexuality is different, which makes him unique in and out of bed.

All men have some things in common and there is no getting around it. Nevertheless, my main focus is geared towards the Black man, because of the various social, psychological and economic factors that have greatly impacted his life and therefore his sexuality. Because of racism, classism, being the man most frequently excluded from his family structure, the first to be discriminated against in the employment sector, the first to be harassed by the law enforcement, etc., the Black man warrants special sensitivity, for he is fragile, yet he is mighty strong. It it's sex you want, stroke the behind. If it's a committed relationship and love, **STROKE THE MIND BEFORE THE BEHIND.**

Haki R. Madhubuti in *Black Man Obsolete, Single, Dangerous?* had the following to say regarding the Black man's status in America:

Therefore, in the United States Black men are still involved in the establishment of significant firsts, such as: first jailed, first killed in the streets, first underemployed, first fired, first confined to mental institutions, first lynched, first involved in drugs and alcohol, first mis-educated, first denied medical treatment, first in suicide, first to be divorced, first to be denied normal benefits of his country, first to be blamed for "Black" problems--indeed, Black men are the first victims.

The book is not addressed to the Black woman solely. For women of every race, creed and color fantasize about being in the arms of a tall, dark, handsome Black male. The movies today continue to depict the Black man as "Mandingo," "Long John" and as a sexual robot, full of energy with everlasting endurance. Unfortunately, Black men have to wade through these myths and stereotyping on their way to the bedroom. Today White women are trying to force themselves through the doors of the Black man's bedroom as a result of these myths and stereotyping. Women around the world fantasize about making love to a Black man. White women are going to great extremes to emulate the Black woman, not excluding her features, in order to share the bed-room with the Black man.

Even today, the size of the Black man's penis and his sexual prowess is the center focus of daily conversations. Many Black men are so obsessed with their penis size and sexual prowess that it causes him to jeopardize his life by refusing to take medications that impact his ability to obtain a long lasting erection.

Dr. Frances Cress Welsing, in the *Isis Paper*, states:

For all that we can imagine doing and all that we will do or fail to do is a result of that picture of "self," derived from our total experiences from birth onward. That picture becomes the basis for all of our behavioral patterns. Unfortunately, a major part of these self and group images for all too many of us Blacks consists of a brief and inaccurate history.

There are challenges that impact the Black man's sexuality. High blood pressure and diabetes is very prevalent among the Black community. Medications taken by men for hypertension sometimes cause impotence. Diabetes is a condition that causes circulation impairment. Poor circulation can have an effect on the erection of the penis. When men do not have an understanding of what is taking place when facing these challenges, they tend to believe it has something to do with their partners ability to arouse them sexually.

They sometimes seek sex from outside the marriage or relationship, hoping to restore their ability to be sexually aroused only to find themselves more frustrated by the increased risk of disrupting their family unit. The Black man is at greater risk of becoming sexually impotent because of socioeconomic factors that impacts his life. These factors impact his life style which causes detrimental damage to his physical and mental health status, therefore his sexuality. The soul food the Black man eats can contribute to impotence because much of the soul food eating facilities cook food high in fats and cholesterol. The following information on low-fat, low-cholesterol diet is from an article entitled "Start A Low-Fat - Low-Cholesterol Diet Now to Prevent Impotency," written by Janet Halbert in the *Natural Healing Newsletter*.

Men! Watching your fat and cholesterol intake now might prevent impotence years down the road.

Researchers in New Zealand discovered that rabbits fed a high-fat, high-cholesterol diet developed impotence from plaque buildup in the arteries of the penis.

And the June 25, 1992 edition of *Medical Tribune* (33,12:14) adds that the same conditions have been found in men with similar diets. Problems from the buildup of plaque in these arteries can be even worse for those whose arteries are already damaged by smoking and high blood pressure. Blockages from cholesterol are one of the chief causes of impotence, the report says.

The stress imposed on the Black man today has taken a toll on his sexuality. Any and all frustration absorbs too much energy. Remember, sexual activities have a strong influence on the way one thinks and performs in all areas of activity.

Black men are finding themselves trying to hide out in the woman's vagina for comfort. They are seeking some form of gratification they have been denied in their work place, etc. Many times the man is too psychologically whipped and stripped to entertain the idea of truly making love to his mate. He finds himself in dying need of a quick high; therefore, all he wants is to have sex. The Black man wants to satisfy his mate sexually. However, he is incapable of doing so at times because of life's circumstances and challenges.

Men have a greater challenge than women when it comes to physical sex. The man has to focus on getting an erection and keeping the erection until his partner is satisfied. This can become a big challenge especially when the woman takes no responsibility for her own desired results. A man becomes embarrassed when he cannot get an erection. He is also embarrassed when he cannot keep an erection. Let me explain my theory for this dilemma.

The Ego Versus Penis Syndrome. With this syndrome, a man is overly anxious not to have a floppy penis before he arrives at home base, therefore during the foreplay the minute he feels a good erection he is ready to put it into the vagina no matter what, because he is unsure as to how long the erection will last. He is obsessed with the idea that he must have an orgasm. He will not ask his partner if she is ready for him. In fact, he cannot bring himself to care at this point about what she is feeling. He is only concerned about his ego and his erected penis at this time. Therefore, he tries to rush his woman into what he is feeling. He may begin by saying words such as, come on baby, I love you ... come on baby, come with me. In order to save his ego when his woman cannot come with him, she fakes it. This syndrome is what has brought about the saying "BIP BAM THANK YOU MA'AM."

Chapter 2

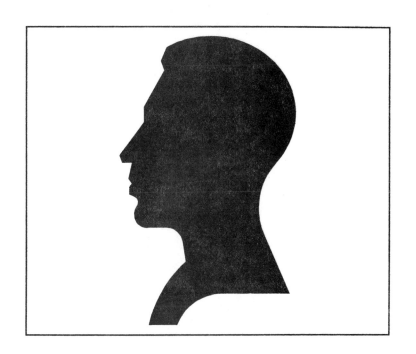

The Effects of Slavery on the Black Man's Sexuality

According to studies, the majority of the slaves brought from Africa settled in the southern states which were slave states. The Black man was socialized not to feel responsible for protecting nor supporting his family. The family worked side by side as partners. Today the Black man is considered less than a man if he cannot provide the lifestyle for his woman that she has seen on television, in books and magazines.

I was reared in the south. I recall many Black men having more than one family. Many Black men had children by many different women. The children were almost always accepted by the father's wife or woman and her children. The women were not fighting each other. The role of a mistress was accepted. Manhood was not based upon monetary status. The male image, disciples, teaching and role modeling were more important benefits to the Black woman than the money he earned.

Chaos ensued as Blacks began to adopt European culture and lifestyles. The Black woman has always been independent and took pride in providing for herself. After slavery, Black women began to say to their daughters, "find you a man that will sit you down," not realizing that the White woman was able to sit down because she had everybody else up. After Slavery, the pressure was on the Black man to protect and support the Black woman. Many Black men abandoned their families because of the guilt and shame they felt as a result of not being able to provide financially. The Social Service Department would only provide for families not intact.

Many Black men abandoned their families because they thought their families would be better off financially with public assistance. As a result of these dilemmas, the Black man began to feel unimportant if he could not provide for his family financially. Delores P. Aldridge, in her book *Focusing Black Male-Female Relationships*, gives and excerpt from Liefour book, *Tally's Corner: A Study of Negro Street Corner Men*, provides this insight:

> The way in which the man makes a living and the kind of living he makes have important consequences for how the man sees himself and is seen by others; and these, in turn importantly shape his relationship with family members, lovers, friends, and neighbors. Making a living takes on an overriding importance at marriage.

> Although he wants to get married he hedges his commitment from the very beginning because he is afraid not of marriage itself, but of his own ability to carry out his responsibilities as a husband and father. His own father failed and had to "cut out" and the men he

knows who have been or are married have also failed or are in the process of doing so. He has no evidence that he will not. The Black menial worker remains a menial worker so that after one or two or three years of marriage and as many children, the man who could not support his family from the very beginning is even less able to support it as time goes on. The longer he works, the longer he is unable to live on what he makes. He has little vested interest in such a job and learns to treat it with the same contempt held for it by the employer and society at large. From his point of view, the job is expendable; from the employer's point of view, he is. Sometimes, he sits down and cries at the humiliation of it all. Sometimes he strikes out at her or the children with his fists, perhaps to lay hallow the claim to being man of the house in the one way left open to him, or perhaps simply to inflict pain on this woman who bears witness to his failure as a husband and father and therefore as a man. Increasingly, he turns to the street corner where a shadow system of values constructed out of public fictions serves to accommodate just such men as he, permitting them to be men once again provided they do not look too closely at one another's credentials (1967:210-213).

As a result of the Black male abandoning his family, the male child was left without the male image and role model. The Black male child orientation and socialization to manhood and sexuality was what he saw on television from people who did not look like him.

Many Black men are not as assertive and aggressive as his mate would want him to be. The Black man has difficulties in those areas because he has been socialized to take the back seat and to demonstrate a low profile when dealing with the female. The Black male environment for the most part consisted of the female gender. The Black man comes from a home most often dominated by a female, a school dominated by females. Usually a younger sister was left in charge to dominate the older male child while his mother was away. The church was the only place, many times, where the Black male child observed men in charge. Maybe that is the reason why we have so many Black preachers and Black churches, for the church is the only institution that Black men have been given freedom to dominate, have power over and control. The Black man is expected to assume a role that he has not been prepared for in most cases. The focus and attention now given to the Black male child today will certainly change and improve the future course for the Black man.

It is important that women understand how these dilemmas impact the Black man's sexuality. Possessing a clear understanding of these dilemmas, women will then be able to embrace the Black man with a deeper love and sensitivity.

The Black man is pressured by the fact that he feels that he has to match up with the sexual script written for him by society. This pressure causes the Black man to cease taking medications prescribed for health conditions such as hypertension, etc. Some medications prescribed for hypertension can cause impotency. When confronted with the option of choosing between the "heart" and the "Hard," many men choose the "Hard." For some men, their manhood and self-image is validated by this thing called "penis." Many men have had heart attacks and strokes because they quit taking their medications. It is sad when a man sacrifices his life for an erected penis.

Chapter 3

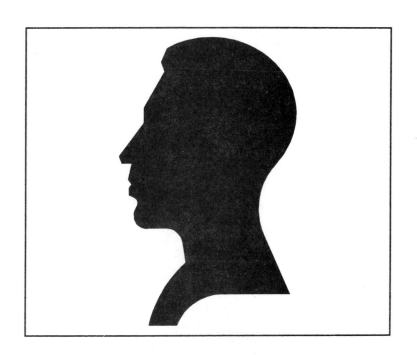

The Kind of Woman a Black Man Wants

The Black man wants a woman who is sensitive to his past, present and future. One who is caring, gentle, thoughtful and respectful.

Sensitive Enough to measure the Black man with the right meter stick. Beginning at the point where he entered the race.

Caring Enough to help him cross over the barriers in his past and present life's experiences that prohibit the enjoyment and gratification of a loving relationship.

Enough to ensure total sexual satisfaction for her Black man.

Gentle Enough to caress with tenderness.

Thoughtful Enough to remember birthdays, anniversaries, etc.

Enough to give a pleasant surprise every now and then.

Enough to help provide financially.
~ Knowing that in today's family many women are in the work place because two incomes are needed.

Thoughtful Enough to make life exciting and exhilarating by:
~ Preparing the bath water.
Laying out a favorite outfit she likes to see her man wear.

Enough to say thank you for things such as:

~ A compliment

~ A romantic evening

~ A good sexual surprise

Respectful Enough to respect a difference of opinion on issues.

The Black man wants a woman who can give to him love, understanding, devotion and respect. The Black man has been deprived of so much; therefore, he tends to want a woman who can be a superwoman. Let me explain just what I mean. He wants a woman to be his wife, his friend, his maid, his children's mother, his mother, his father and his protector.

The Black man wants a woman who understands how slavery and racism impacts his life today. He wants a woman to understand that he is the victim and not the perpetrator of the conditions he finds himself in today.

As Don Spears in his book *In Search of GOODPUSSY* so eloquently stated:

> What Black men really need is not to be blamed for problems they did not create. For example, Black men are blamed for not working, when they are not doing the hiring. Black men are accused of being lazy, worthless no accounts, when their blood and sweat built this country.

He wants a woman who understands the various social, psychological and economical factors that have impacted his life, his ability to bond, his self-esteem and therefore his sexuality.

The Black man wants a woman who can look beyond the negative media reports regarding the future forecast for 25% of Black men and can lend praises to the 75% that you never read or hear about. Andrew Billingsley, Ph.D. in *Climbing Jacob's Ladder* wrote the following:

> There are more Black adults who have graduated from high school and who know how to read and write than there are Black high school dropouts. There are three times as many Black youths who have managed to stay out of the criminal justice system than the celebrated 25 percent who have become engulfed in it.

Earl Ofari Hutchinson, Ph.D. wrote in *The Assassination of The Black Male Image*:

> We have been constantly reminded that absentee Black men have turned Black families into a "tangle of pathology." Bill Clinton, George Bush and Dan Quayle made the family a big issue during the 1992 presidential campaign. Conservatives use it as a battering ram against the evils of welfarism and big government.
>
> *Newsweek* in a cover story feature dredged up the issue and blamed the sorry plight of the ghetto on "A World Without Fathers." Anyone can make a compelling case for the Black male deviance and family destabilization.
>
> Here's how. Jumble income and population figures, downplay the achievements of the Black middle-class, ignore the profound gender role changes in American society; then pretend that the Reagan-Bush cuts in job, education, and family support programs benefitted the poor.

The Black man wants a woman who recognizes that even today, as in the past, the behavior and various configurations of the Black family are a direct response, adaptation and reflection of the society around him. Statistics given regarding the number of households headed by the female in the Black community is supposed to be a negative reflection on the Black man.

Andrew Hacker in *Two Nations* says:

The pool of "marriageable" Black men gets smaller every year. A traditional requisite for marriage has been having a steady job or the prospect of one, a status not readily achieved given current unemployment rates.

The Black man wants a woman who does not expect him to be a caucasian-clone. A woman who realizes that he has a history, belief system and values of his own. A woman who does not measure him by the white man's standards and his behaviors.

The Black man needs and wants a woman who can love him and who can teach him how to openly express love. A woman who can help him feel the joy of bonding. He wants a woman who makes him feel very special in bed and out of bed. He wants a woman who can make him laugh and one who can accept him when he must also cry. A woman who will listen to him, one who believes in him, one who encourages him. A woman who wants to be his friend and companion. A woman who loves him when he is not capable of loving himself. One who can reach out to him and also show him how to reach out to her. A woman who understands that his hidden emotions and his inability to express love is a result of generational perpetuation. He wants a woman who is willing to give of herself to help break the perpetuating pain that enslaves his emotions.

The Black man wants a woman who knows how and when to pamper him. In fact, out of all he has been through and is still going through he justifiably deserves all the pampering one can give to him.

Below is a list of ways to pamper and to show affection to your Black man. Remember, it is easier for a man to ask for sex than it is to ask for love and affection. This list will teach you how to give your Black man what he wants and needs---intimacy. Intimacy helps to open those blocked channels and allows energy to flow into areas that have been closed for years due to past hurt and pain.

Nothing on this list is expensive, nor time consuming. In fact, most of the things on the list will not impact your finances. It is sometimes difficult for one to start doing things he or she has not done before in a relationship. The question becomes, what is he going to think? Is he going to think that someone is teaching me new tricks. Relieve yourself of those anxieties and get busy pampering and loving your Black man.

If you practice the following list of suggestions, your Black man will keep returning to your table for a great feast and you will have him eating out of the palm of your hand.

1. Spend intimate time with your partner.
2. Take responsibility for your sexual satisfaction.
3. Be his friend.
4. Be honest with him.
5. Encourage him to be honest with you.
6. Trust him.
7. Praise him for the good he does.
8. Tell him and show him that you appreciate him.
9. Forgive him for mistakes and don't keep bring ing it up over and over again.
10. Respect him and show him respect.
11. Respect his opinion even when you do not agree with it.
12. Listen to him.
13. Compliment him on his achievements.
14. Brag on him to your relatives and friends in his presence.
15. Send him flowers.
16. Make sure that he has peace at home.
17. Compliment him when he is wearing your favorite cologne.
18. Tell him the outfit you like seeing him wear.
19. Give him a manicure and pedicure.
20. Give him a body massage.
21. Limit your time on the phone when he is with you.

22. Accept his friends.
23. Encourage him to be a part of his children' lives.
24. Ask for his opinion.
25. Take him on surprise outings.
26. Allow him to have female friends.
27. Do not talk about your past relationships with other men.
28. Do not ask him about prior women in his life if you cannot deal with the truth.
29. When you are wrong apologize.
30. Remember and help to celebrate his family and friend commemorations.
31. Pray with him.
32. Always show respect for his parents.
33. Encourage him to eat healthy.
34. Encourage him to have annual medical check ups.
35. If he becomes impotent reassure him and help him overcome it.
36. Do not talk about him to his relatives nor his friends.
37. Prepare his bath water.
38. Lay out his favorite lingerie.
39. Wear your lingerie that he likes best.
40. Sleep in the nude sometimes.
41. Serve him meals in bed.
42. Take baths and showers with him.

43. Tell him what's on your mind, but don't nag.
44. Believe in him.
45. Flirt with him.
46. Pat him on the buttocks.
47. Watch TV with him.
48. Offer to drive him, when he seems tired.
49. Pay attention to his clothes.
50. Make sure that his shoes look good.
51. Buy him clothes.
52. Pack love notes in his lunch.
53. Give him gift certificates.
54. Encourage him to read.
55. Do not remind him of his failure.
56. Have a party at home, just the two of you.
57. Give him space.
58. Respect his private time.
59. Be sexually creative.
60. Tease him.
61. Tell him he is sexy.
62. You be sexy.
63. Wear his favorite cologne.
64. Learn how to shave him.
65. Brush his hair.
66. Teach him to prepare a good meal.
67. Brag on his cooking.
68. Allow him to take a mini-vacation without you.
69. Do not try to change him.
70. Communicate--communicate--communicate!

71. Tell him exactly what's on your mind.
72. Allow him to tell you what's on his mind.
73. Do not judge him.
74. Do not contradict him in public.
75. When you are wrong, apologize and mean it.
76. Tell him everyday and in everyway that you love him.

Then why is it so difficult for the Black man to open up to his woman and children? I will conclude this chapter with the words of an author who has written the only such book of its kind that examines every aspect of the Black man entitled, *In Search of GOODPUSSY Living Without Love. The Real Truth About Men and Their Relationships.*

I believe that at least part of the answer to those questions may be historic.

BLACKS WHO WERE CONSIDERED LESS THAN HUMAN WERE NOT PERMITTED TO DISPLAY POSITIVE HUMAN EMOTIONS. Slaves whose children were sold were often whipped if they cried. Again, fathers produced new laborers, not closely knit families with which to form loving bonds. If anything, it was better not to form attachments at all for loved ones who might be sold or killed by night fall. On larger plantations even mothers did not have primary care of their young. That was the role of the mammy. BLACK PEOPLE, WHO WERE SUPPOSED TO BE ANIMALS WITHOUT SOULS OR HEARTS, SEEM TO HAVE BEEN BRAINWASHED INTO BELIEVING THAT THEY REALLY WERE NOT SENSITIVE, CARING HUMAN BEINGS.

Even shame probably played its role, as in instances of humiliation. Suppose, for example, that one of the young females was taken out at night and sexually abused by the master. The only real way to deal with such deep emotional issues was to deny or suppress them. The best way to cover up the shame was to pretend that nothing really happened, because the slave was powerless to do anything about it anyway. Their true feelings were perhaps so real, so passionate, that the only natural instinct would have been to kill.

TODAY BLACK PEOPLE STILL SEEM TO BE SUPPRESSING THEIR FEELINGS, EVEN FROM THEMSELVES, UNLESS THEY ARE IN SOME BAPTIST CHURCH OR AT A WAKE OR A FUNERAL. They seem to need a reason or an excuse before they can open up and let whatever is inside come out. This is truly tragic because Black and Brown people are as warm and loving inside as the tropical climate that kindly nurtured them.

Now that you understand the Black man's past, present and future journey, you can appreciate him, respect him, and love him in a way that you have never loved him before.

Chapter 4

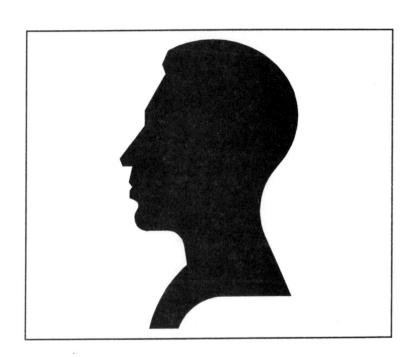

What the Black
Man Wants
From His
Woman in Bed

As a whole, the Black man wants love, trust, respect and sensitivity from his woman or lover. He wants a physical and emotional communion that enhances and deepens love. Among other things, he seeks pleasure, closeness, reassurance, comfort, release from tension, and escape. Many Black men do not find it easy to ask for what they want from their women; they expect her to read their mind and to know what they need. Let me further explain. Many Black men find it easy to ask for sex, however, they are starved for love and they have difficulty asking for it.

The Black man does not want to be compared with other men. they do not want to have to feel as though they are a performer when in bed. The Black man needs to know that his woman sees his worth far beyond his penis. In fact, the real secret is that many Black men would prefer more love and less sex. Much of this sex business is really about what he feels that his woman expects from him. He feels that his woman would suffer disappointment if he does not aggressively seek intercourse with her. Do not read me wrong, Black men do love sex and it is the only form of gratification within reach for many of them. For many Black men the only avenue of escape from the pressures of this society has been the "two W's"--Wine and Women. It dates back to slavery, the only encounter that the Black man had that reinforced his manhood was his juicy sexual encounter with his woman.

There are many stereotypical statements that have been perpetuated regarding the Black man's sexuality. One stereotype in particular is that Black men need more sex than other men. This is the reason for the saying that you have heard down through the years: "If you want to punish a Black man, take away his p---y." This is only the case for those Black men who are deprived of other forms of gratification due to various social and economical factors.

The Black man wants more than sex in bed. He wants caressing, conversation, plenty of fun, romance, surprises and understanding. I guess you are saying "understanding, what is there to understand while in bed with a Black man other than the fact that he is going to set your soul on fire." Well, he needs you to understand that he is not Mandingo, he is not Long John, he is not the ever-ready battery full of energy and endurance. When he crawls up in your arms in bed he has more on his mind than sex. Therefore, you should ask him, honey what are your needs tonight? You should also tell him what you want and need from him. After all, the Black man wants a woman who takes the initiative for romance and sex. Don Spears made the following statement:

> Women do not take the initiative often enough so it's wonderful when you find one who does, who just wants to please you sometimes without expecting anything in return.

The Black man wants a woman who can ask for what she wants from him in bed. For he does not want to try to read her mind. He wants a woman who can take responsibility for her own sexual gratification instead of making him alone be responsible.

You must remember that the Black man has been put down so much on a daily basis, that he needs much reassurance and validation. The Black man will say words to his woman during intercourse such as, "baby is this big dick good to you or do you like this big dick, etc." This is because he seeks sexual validation. The Black man's large penis is the one thing that he has been given world recognition for.

The Black man wants a woman who is sensitive to him enough to know when he is not conducive to providing her good sex, nor capable of receiving romance nor providing her with romance. These times do come in a man's life, particularly and more often in the Black man's life.

Impotency is on the rise among African American men, as a result of the disease process of diabetes, the effects from medications used for hypertension, substance abuse as a means to escape the pain of reality, stress brought on by the effects of racism coupled with economic deprivations and the lack of energy and stamina due to depression.

Dr. Jack Ende, M.D., is his article, "Screening for Sexual Dysfunction" in *Medical Aspects of Human Sexuality* made this observation:

> Sexual dysfunction may be a clue to depression or, alternatively, be its cause. In either case, data on sexual dysfunction may explain important psychological problems.

Steven L. Dubonsky, M.D. in his article, "When Sexual Dysfunction Masks Anxiety and Depression" in *Medical Aspects of Human Sexuality* reminds readers:

> Patients with depression and/or anxiety often suffer from sexual dysfunction. Sexual problems may result from loss of the capacity to experience pleasure, inhibited sexual desire, loss of libido, distraction, performance anxiety, or adverse effects of self treatment with alcohol or other depressants. Marital and relationship problems are even more common as the depressed and/or

anxious patient becomes unavailable, dependent, complaining or irritable.

Clinton W. Young, M.D. and Daniel Wlodarczyk, M.D. in their article, "Counseling the Impotent Man with Diabetes" in *Medical Aspects of Human Sexuality* made the following observation:

> Impotence is a common complaint among diabetic patients: Roughly half of the approximate 5 million American male patients with diabetes suffer from impotence. There has been some controversy regarding this point, however, since some researchers believe that diabetic neuropathy is the usual cause of diabetic impotence. "Patients with diabetic impotence often also suffer from various degrees of guilt and depression, which may compound the problems."

The Black man needs his woman to feel good about helping him restore sexual potency. He wants a woman who will seek alternative ways of providing for herself and for her man's sexual pleasure in the absence of an erected penis. He likes to be held, kissed and caressed. He also enjoys romance without sex. He does not want to be viewed as a sexual stud or a piece of meat.

It is important that a woman understands the sexual challenges that a man faces today as related to his sexuality. I will discuss male impotency to help you gain a better insight as impotency is so prevalent today. Men are very reluctant to seek help for sexual dysfunctions, they would rather believe that their woman is the problem. I will also share with you ways in which you may help your man overcome problems such as premature ejaculation and erectile dysfunction.

Impotence used to be considered the lot that awaited the middle aged and elderly; however, today, we know that age is not as much a factor as you think. We are seeing more of it in younger men as well.

Impotence is the failure to achieve erection, ejaculation or both. Men who experience sexual dysfunction express the following complaints: loss of sexual desire, not being able to obtain or maintain an erection, ejaculatory failure, premature ejaculation and the inability to achieve orgasm.

In the past impotence was considered to be 90 percent in a man's head. Because of ignorance, many men today do not seek medical help for impotency. It is now believed that the majority of impotent men have a component of underlying organic disease. Some common causes of erectile impotence and lack of sexual desire in men are boredom, resentment, anger, grief, anxiety, depression, diabetes and prescription drugs such as antihypertensives (used for treating high blood pressure), antidepressants (used for treating depression and anxiety), anticholinergic (used for treating ulcers) and drugs of habituation or addiction such as alcohol, methadone, cocaine, heroin and marijuana.

An erection for a man is equivalent to lubrication for a woman. The male erection and female lubrication both signify readiness for intercourse. A man cannot have intercourse if he does not have an erection, but a woman does not have to lubricate in order to have intercourse. It can be uncomfortable if she does not lubricate, but there are ways around that. Saliva or a lubricator may be used.

Some experts believe that we are seeing more impotence in men today because the modern day woman is demanding equal joy in sex. Women are educated consumers regarding sex. More is being written about sex and women are speaking out on national television talk shows and other media. Woman are now more sexually aggressive and feel entitled to sexual satisfaction and demand it. This assertiveness of the modern day female has created performance anxiety among men. Many men entering into a sexual experience are afraid that they may not meet the woman's expectations.

Those anxieties can cause problems such as impotence. The big "O" (orgasm) is the talk of the time; therefore, men are feeling pressured to guarantee women an orgasmic experience every time during sexual intercourse.

It is important for a male to have a thorough physical examination if he has demonstrated little or no interest in sex for a long period of time. A man's impotence is said to be psychological if he is able to get an erection by masturbating or looking at pornography, has early morning erections and if he can have an erection with another woman.

Intermittent impotence has been found to be caused by an endocrine imbalance. Endocrine problems are very sneaky. Their only symptom may be that of impotence. A man experiencing impotence should ask his doctor to check his testosterone level. Testosterone is a male hormone. A man has an erection when blood floods through the penile arteries into the blood vessels in the penis. This rush of blood is triggered by the nervous system, which gets its signal from the sex hormones.

Impotence can be a symptom of a number of life threatening diseases. It is one of the symptoms of diabetes because diabetes can cause impaired circulation. Remember, a good erection is a good blood flow to the penis. Diabetes may damage or destroy the nerves that triggers the rush of blood to the penis. According to research, more than three hundred thousand men a year are diagnosed with diabetes. More than half of them are or may be impotent. Impotency caused by diabetes is usually not curable.

Premature Ejaculation This disorder seldom has an organic cause. It is usually related to anxiety in the sexual situation, unreasonable expectations about performance, or an emotional disorder. Black men are burdened with sexual stereotyping regarding their sexuality. They have been labeled as "Mandingo," "Long John" and "Eveready Battery." The Black man takes these burdens to the bedroom. Therefore, he is pressured more to be an excellent performer in bed.

Men are concerned most about the size of their penis. The size of the penis provokes much anxiety for the male. The average penis is three to four inches long and grows to six inches or so when erected. Most men do not know that the circumference of the penis is more important when it comes to a woman's pleasure. The thicker the penis, the more it will stimulate the clitoris and the lower third of the vagina during intercourse, as this is where the greatest sensations come from.

It is believed that more men suffer from premature ejaculation than from impotence. A premature ejaculator may ejaculate as soon as his penis enters the vagina. Some even start on the way in. All men have experienced premature ejaculation at one time or another. It happens to young men engaging in sexual intercourse for the first time almost always. Men with experience come too soon sometimes because of intense excitement, anxiety or fatigue.

The man who is considered a true premature ejaculator is the man who comes too soon every time or almost every time he makes love. This is a very humiliating, devastating and embarrassing situation for a man.

Some men are considerate, thoughtful and loving enough to compensate for this dilemma by bringing their partner to orgasm before they become aroused or at least before entering the vagina. Some men cease having intercourse with their wives and partners.

During my research, I discovered that the majority of men who suffer from premature ejaculation do not try to compensate for their sexual dysfunction. Some women who are married to premature ejaculators stated that their men do not even kiss them or caress them in any fashion. The majority of these men will not seek medical help and many of them are in denial and blame their mate for their sexual dysfunction.

I also discovered that those women who were in touch with their own sexuality were able to ask for what they want and need sexually from their men in spite of their impotency and premature ejaculation. These were much happier women. Those women who could not ask for what they wanted because of their fear of rejection and fear of hurting their partner's ego felt angry, abused, frustrated and used. These feelings were a result of their partner not discussing the dilemma and by acting as though they thought everything was all right. These women sometimes walked out of the relationship without giving any reason for doing such.

Chapter Eleven in my book, *Satisfying the Black Woman Sexually Made Simple*, deals with a recipe for sexual fulfillment. This chapter will enlighten and enhance a man's knowledge and his ability to give much pleasure to his mate with or without an erected penis.

Many marriages have been broken up because of premature ejaculation. It is important for men and women to know that premature ejaculation can be cured. A couple must be willing to work together to make it a shared experience. As a result of this, the couple will grow closer together with a more enjoyable and gratifying sexual relationship and the cure will be more effective. Cure meaning when a man can prevent himself from ejaculating until he and his partner are both satisfied at least most of the time.

The Black man wants a woman who is willing to help him through sexual crises. Sexual difficulty spills over into every aspect of one's life and activities. Remember that, next to eating, good sex is the most sought after experience by humans.

I have found it helpful in discussing masturbation as a prelude or prerequisite to premature ejaculation control technique. One must accept the idea that it is OK to touch the penis and to manipulate it for self pleasure without a feeling of guilt, shame and that of being abnormal. His sexual partner must also become comfortable with the touching and manipulation of the penis without feeling responsible or inadequate because of his sexual dysfunction.

The real truth is that women have now been given the OK for self masturbation. Men have not been given the green light. However, most men do masturbate on a regular basis. Masturbation for men, unlike masturbation for women, has nothing to do with their partner's availability nor their partner's ability to give them sexual satisfaction.

Most women would like to believe that adolescent boys are the only males who masturbate and that they cease masturbation once they find themselves girlfriends. Nicholas Martin said in *All Hands on Dick*: "Now, if a man says, I'd give my right arm, you'll know he's lying." You see most men are right-handed; therefore, their right hands are used for masturbation.

My research on sexual behavior has led me to agree with other researchers. Many leading authorities believe that premature ejaculation seen in many men could stem from the frequent "quickies" they have been giving themselves as far back as boyhood.

When men begin masturbation they feel a need to do it quickly as not to be caught, after all it is not an acceptable "normal" thing to do. Even in the age of free sexual expressions, the caring and sharing decade, masturbation is one area of a man's life that only few couples discuss, and still today only a few women understand it.

The following is a brief history of masturbation according to Nicholas Martin from *All Hands on Dick*:

The Greeks took a blase view of masturbation. Hippocrates said it was a waste of time which could be better spent thinking.

The Romans shared a similar view but believed it to be a waste of sexual energy which could be more enjoyably spent in orgies.

In 1776 the Swiss doctor, Tissot, wrote a pamphlet entitled *The Heinous Sin of Self Pollution* about the frightful consequences of this abominable practice. No doubt based on the belief that sperm was produced in the head, he claimed to have proof that masturbation reduced the size of the brain.

Unfortunately, in 1778, the Pope took all this seriously and ordered the Alpine quack to Rome, where he persuaded His Holiness that masturbation was also the cause of an epidemic of typhoid sweeping through Italy at the time. The Pope laid down the law and anyone found masturbating was beaten in the streets.

In 1850 masturbation became more than a medical problem, it became a moral one too. The genitals were viewed as being "in a state of constant rebellion" against God, and the biblical story of Onan (a man who was struck down after shedding his seed on the ground) was used to terrify young people into abstention.

This interpretation of the story has passed onto this day and gives rise to the expression "Onanist," though it's a classic example of history being rewritten. Anyone can see that Onan's story is an example of coitus interruptus.

In 1900 doctors developed even more cruel methods with which to "cure" people of masturbation. Scalding of the genitals became popular, as did "infibulation"--the piercing of the penis with a steel pin or, in women, the removal of the clitoris. Metal splints were sold to parents to attach to their sons' genital to prevent arousal.

However, probably the most psychologically disturbing device that the twisted Victorian mind ever devised was the "alarm." When a young man got an erection during the night, a bell would ring to alert his parents, who could then run in to make sure he wasn't masturbating. Pavlov, eat your heart out.

So why do Black men masturbate? Remember, I stated earlier that all men have some things in common and masturbation is one of those things that Black men have in common with all other men. They masturbate because it is a normal healthy thing to do. They like it, it feels good and it is sexually gratifying. Masturbation also provides man a sense of independence and control. Masturbation is by no means a substitute for intercourse. It is separate and unique. Some men have described it as being more akin to meditation than making love. Don Spears explains this about Black men and masturbation:

> Masturbation is quick, it's cheap and it's probably the safest sex you can have, and although many Black men do it during their lifetime, you will almost never hear them bragging about it. Most of the adult Black males I talked to who admitted that they masturbate said that they do it because they know better than anyone else what makes them feel good and because they hated the idea of depending on someone else all the time for sexual gratification. Some of them love to have their wives or their girlfriends instead of "jerking off," while others said that masturbating was a fair trade when females either held back or were not available. Some Black men felt that they had the right to please themselves if their partners could not or would not satisfy them, and that masturbation actually kept them from pressuring their women for sex sometimes.

Now that you understand a little more about the male penis and its sensitivity to the hand touching, you are in better position to help him to feel sexually whole again.

Let us discuss ways to help the male who cannot obtain an erected penis. If it is due to a medical reason, then, there is nothing that you can do as his partner to stimulate an erection. However, there are things that you can do to give him sexual pleasure and make him feel like a man. It is important for a woman to be in touch with her own sexuality so that she can teach her man how to give her sexual pleasure in the absence of an erected penis. More is discussed on the mechanics of providing sexual pleasure in Chapter 9 on Recipe for Sexual Fulfillment. To help men better understand ways to explore the women's erogenous zones I have included excerpts from my book *Satisfying The Black Woman Sexually Made Simple*.

Massage the ear lobes gently in a circular motion. Guide the tongue over the surface of the ear lobe, softly sucking the ear lobe in between a fixed number of glides, then, blow small puffs of soothing warm air over the wet surface of each ear lobe.

Give special attention to the nipples. The nipples should be handled with delicacy for good stimulation and excitation. If you are rough with the nipples it will cause pain and pain will cause the muscles to contract. Remember, your sole objective is total relaxation. Now over the nipples glide your tongue in a circular motion clockwise then counter clockwise. Then with medium pressure blow warm air over the wet surface of the nipples.

If the breasts are large pull the nipple close together and caress both at the same time. If the breasts are small, go from one to the other stimulating interchangeably in a circular motion with light pressure. Remember, the size of the breast is not an issue.

When you hit the hot spot you will notice a drastic change in her breathing pattern. Move away from that hot spot and search for other areas to explore. Every now and then come back to that hot spot for another burst of pleasure.

Massage the body beginning with the feet. Before massaging the feet, apply a generous amount of oil over the palms of your hands. Start at the tip of the toes and work towards the heel. This usually relaxes the whole body.

Massage the legs with light strokes proceeding in an upward and downward motion, moving from ankle to knee and from knee to ankle. Massage the thigh lightly with circular and crossing strokes.

Lightly massage the belly button. Gently massage the pubic area with one hand while the other hand is massaging the nipples of the breast.

Very gently lubricate the clitoral and vaginal area with Vaseline or KY jelly etc. Glide your finger over the glands of the clitoris. Place your thumb and first finger over the glands of the clitoris. Very, very softly open and close your fingers. Remember always to be tender but yet, sensitive to her response including increasing and decreasing in the frequency and intensity of the stimulation of various areas according to her body language, expression and vocal gestures.

A woman can help her man overcome psychogenic impotency. (Impotency that is not caused by medical conditions.) Few events in a man's life can trigger stronger reactions of humiliation, shame and self-blame than does impotency. Impotency can affect a man to a degree where he may feel inhibited from seeking professional counselling. Dr. Ruth said in her book *Guide To Erotic & Sensuous Pleasures*, about erectile difficulties:

Men are often the victims of a Catch-22 situation when it comes to their erectile difficulties. You see, they are worried that they may have a problem because they are not performing satisfactorily (at least not up to their own standards). Then, the stress this worry produces may cause them to perform poorly because stress is often the cause of erectile problems in many men. In other words, the concern that they may have some difficulties with an erection can actually cause the difficulty. This is sometimes called a "self-fulfilling prophecy" or "antici-patory anxiety." It seems that so many people are always fighting with themselves doesn't it?

When a man does experience any type of sexual dysfunction, it is wise to encourage him to see a doctor. Sometimes sexual dysfunction is the first symptom of some physiological problems. There are a few tests that the two of you can do to determine whether this problem is in his mind or in his apparatus. According to Dr. Ruth "If you want a simple, but not necessarily fool-proof, test to see if you do have erections in your sleep, take the "stamp test." Buy a roll of postage stamps from the post office. When you are ready to retire, take about 5 to 8 stamps in a strip and run it snugly around the base of your penis. Place a little moisture on the end of the last stamp so that they will stay in place during the night. Go to sleep and have pleasant dreams. If the strip of stamps is split when you get up in the morning you probably had a good stiff erection."

Also, if your man can achieve an erection via mastur-bation, pornography magazines or movies or with another woman, there is nothing wrong with his appara-tus. It is time for communication between the two of you and it is time for counselling.

John E. Nelson M.D., in an article in *Medical Aspects of Human Sexuality* entitled "Counseling the Female Partner of A Man with Psychogenic Impotence" states:

> It is normal for a man to be unable to function sexually from time to time and it is just one of those things men have to learn to live with.

Helping your man overcome premature ejaculation. Your man can overcome this problem if he is open minded and willing. You can help by demonstrating love and care instead of showing frustration. You should never ignore the problem hoping it will go away. In most cases it becomes worse, because of the anxieties associated with it. Express to your man all the things that you enjoy about his romance and lovemaking. Share with him that there are exercises that he can do by himself to learn ejaculation control and that there are exercises that the two of you can share together to help him to be in control. Assure him of your love and your willingness to help him achieve his sexual goal. Most of all, be patient and supportive. Please do not bring him a book on the subject and just leave it where he can see or read it. Do not discuss his problems with others, you never know who knows who and who, talks to who. Your bedroom business should not become "hard copy" nor "current affairs."

I will now discuss ejaculatory control (premature ejaculation). According to research, about one third of all men suffer from an inability to control the timing of when they will ejaculate. What is ejaculatory control? I like the way Bernie Zilbergeld, Ph.D. explains it:

> While ejaculation is a reflex and can't be controlled perfectly, a man who has developed control can enjoy high levels of sexual arousal, whether from oral or manual stimulation or intercourse, without coming, and he usually has a choice when to ejaculate. He can allow his arousal to rise to a high level and then more or less level off until he wants to come.

The time it takes to gain ejaculatory control varies from man to man. Some factors to be considered are attitude, patience, willingness, eagerness of the male to satisfy his partner, and feelings regarding masturbation. Some experts believe that one can expect to gain control within 2-8 weeks when self-motivated.

On the following page is a physical sexual response phases chart of men's and women's dysfunctions. This chart was taken from Gina Ogden, Ph.D. book entitled *Sexual Recovery*.

		Symptom of Sexual Dysfunction	
Response Phase	Primary Neuro-physiological Mechanism	Women's	Men's
Desire	Limbic system and other sexual centers in brain-- send pleasure messages to central nervous system.	Low desire	Low desire
Excitement	Parasympathetic nervous system in spinal column-- sends message for vasodilation direct to genitals (not under your control).	Lack of lubrication	Impotence
Orgasm	Sympathetic nervous system in spinal column-- sends message direct to genitals (partly under your control).	Anorgasmia	Premature ejaculation

Table 3.   Physical Sexual Response Phases and Men's and Women's Dysfunction

I believe that in order for a woman to totally satisfy her man she must understand the male sexual responses. Now that you have a better understanding regarding male sexual dysfunction, you can now learn ways to help him overcome his problems, particularly premature ejaculation.

Ejaculation Control Techniques. You should begin by touching and stimulating for pleasure. This should not lead to sexual intercourse. The penis is not to be inserted into the vagina. The build-up of long-term blood engorgement due to repeated and prolonged sexual stimulation and excitation may cause pain in the testicles and penis. If your man experiences pain and discomfort, you can help bring him to ejaculation via masturbation.

Stop and Start Techniques. Whether masturbating is done by your man or by you, the friction is to cease when he feels the urge to come. Allow him to hold still and the two of you may just want to converse about what he was feeling. Start the process over again. After three sessions on the start and stop exercise, allow him to ejaculate outside the vagina. Do this exercise daily for seven consecutive days. If you detect that your man is not conducive to good sex or is not in the right frame of mind, do not attempt the exercise for that day. For it has been said by the wise that good sex doesn't mix with stress, tension and anxiety. It is important for your man to understand that you are not to be left out while he is learning control. He must give you pleasure and stimulate you to orgasm by whatever means the two of you agree upon.

One may wonder why it is that the man cannot tell when he is about to come. Dr. Ruth made the following observations.

Why is it that so many men seem unaware of this momentary lag between the beginning of the orgasmic sensation and its heightening during ejaculation? It is not too difficult to understand. For most men, orgasm is the goal of sexual activity, not the sensations along the way. These men have never been trained to become sensitive to the different sensations of the orgasm and are largely unaware that there is still time to control the process.

These exercises are a learning process, and most men will not pick up this new skill of self control in just one or two sessions. When the man does ejaculate unintentionally, talk to him about how it felt just before the onset of the orgasmic stage. Turn the minor failure into a major lesson so that he can better recognize these sensations the next time.

Now that your man is successful with the stop and start exercises, you can take him to a higher level. Begin by lying on top of him with the penis in the vagina. Your man is to lie passively as you move up and down. You may also use your pubococcygeal muscle by tightening and relaxing the muscle to stimulate the penis instead of moving up and down on the penis. This method is just as effective. When your man feels the sensation to come he will tell you to stop. His penis will remain inside you until you are ready to begin stimulation again. After practicing your stop and start exercises successfully for a few times, your man will tell you when to continue doing what you are doing as he has now gained a vote of confidence. See illustration of the male penis.

Squeeze Technique. Apply the squeeze method technique used for controlling premature ejaculation. The penile squeeze is a very effective method of delaying ejaculation. It is used by almost every sex therapist and has been proven to work. Place your thumb on the frenulum of the penis, with two fingers on the back side, one above the coronal ridge and the other below the coronal ridge. Squeeze tightly and have him tighten his PC muscles a few seconds before the moment of inevitability. This will inhibit his ejaculatory reflex. Maintain the squeeze for ten to twenty seconds or until the urge to come subsides.

This picture is an excerpt from the book *One Hour Orgasm*.

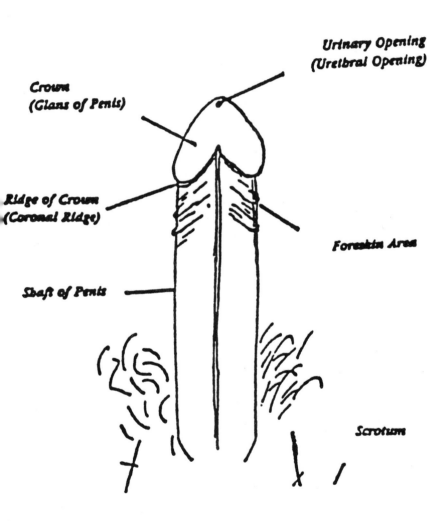

The following photos were taken from the book *Touching For Pleasure*.

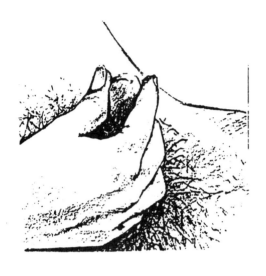

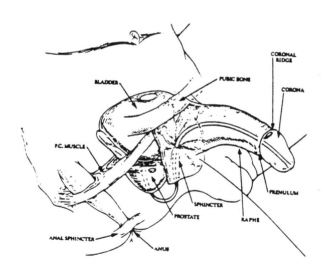

When your man ejaculates too soon or shall I say before you are satisfied, do not frustrate him by trying to stimulate him to obtain a second erection. This can be quite embarrassing and humiliating for the man who has a slow recovery time. The recovery period (refractory period) may be hours for some and days for others and just minutes for the young man. The refractory time has to do with mind set and also the ability of the body to regenerate the seminal fluids necessary for ejaculation. Therefore, if you are in need of a relief after your man has ejaculated, suggest methods of getting what you want without the use of his penis. If the penis is what he proceeds to give you more of, then peace be unto you.

If you fully understand all that you have read and if you put it all into practice, I guarantee you that your Black man ain't going nowhere but back to you as often as he can.

The following is a list of responses that I gathered from a two year survey of 1,000 Black men, professional and non-professional, with the age range of 19 to 65.

What words do you enjoy hearing?

"Oh daddy give me that big dick"

"Baby I love you, but I hate it when they ask me do

I love them. I feel like it is the wrong time to ask for truth, plus I feel taken advantage of when asked such a question during lovemaking "Baby give it all to me" "It's not the words, it's the moans and groans as long as it is coming naturally I don't care"

Have women ever asked you what turns you on?

"I've never had a woman to ask me."

"I guess women think that we are so simple after all, all Black men are supposed to stay ready for sex, bullshit"

Most men said that women do not ask what turns them on.

Have you ever desired more foreplay before sex?

"I would appreciate any attempt. Women have to understand that just because a man has an erection doesn't mean that he is ready for lovemaking. An erection is a simple biological response. Anything can cause an erection. Body-builders on stage sometimes get them. Men get them when they are asleep, or watching sporting events, or for no particular reason at all."

The majority of men answered yes to desiring more

foreplay. I guess women are reading men's readiness incorrectly.

What do you say to your partner when you experience premature ejaculation?

"Blessed at my age to experience it at all"

"Never really thought about how I feel"

"Sometimes I feel bad, depending on the person and whether I am trying to satisfy her or myself only"

"I feel very bad and sometimes I never call the woman again"

"You feel like a real asshole"

"Oh it is awful"

Do you like your partner to express herself verbally during sexual intercourse?

Most men answered yes to this question.

Name the times, circumstances or happening when you are not conducive to good sex, (meaning when you cannot put your all into it)

"When I am tired"

"When I am angry"

"When I am overly stressed"

"When my money ain't right"

How do you feel when you have had an argument or provoked to anger and your mate wants to have sex before resolving the matter?

"I feel we should have sex and settle this argument, then have another argument so we can settle that one also"

"We can talk but argue by yourself"

"I am not very happy when this happens. I perform, I will not deny her what she wants, but my mind is on the situation"

"I usually don't unless I wanted to before the argument started"

Do you enjoy having oral sex performed on you?

71% answered yes

29% answered no

Do you enjoy performing oral sex?

35% answered yes

65% answered no

Are you self conscious about the size of your penis?

45% said yes

55% said no

One man answered, "How can you not be with all the talk about the Black man's penis size"

Do you masturbate?

70% answered yes

30% answered no

If yes, why?

"Yes, but not anymore, I'm married"

"No, that would be selfish"

"It allows me the pleasure to do what I want"

"I can be selfish without feeling guilty"

"The orgasm is more pleasurable and powerful"

"I can pretend I am with whomever I want to be with. It is fun"

What part of your penis is most sensuous?

"Head"

Most answers were the head of the penis.

What stimulates you the most causing an erection?

"Touching the head of my penis"

"Breath of warm air on my penis head"

"Oral sex"

"Watching my woman walk"

"Holding my penis tightly"

"Thoughts, good ones"

"Naked photo of my woman"

Do you wear condoms?

60% answered no

40% answered yes

If your answer is no, explain why?

"Does not feel the same"

"I usually only see one woman at a time"

"My woman and I are only seeing each other"

"I only screw high class women"

"My wife and I are disease free, clean and she can have no children"

Name your sensuous spots (hot buttons)

"Neck, chest and thigh"

"Ear, back of neck"

"Penis head"

"Nipples, neck, earlobes"

"Inner thigh, near my scrotum"

What hot button do most women tend to go to?

"My lips"

"Neck"

"If at all, just the penis"

Is it important to marry a virgin?

75% answered no

25% answered yes

What are some of your sexual fantasies?

"Having sex in the pool"

"Having sex hanging upside down"

"Having sex in an air balloon"

"Having sex with 3 women"

"Having sex in the car"

When your mate is having a sexual affair with another man, do you think it has something to do with what you're doing or not doing?

80% answered no

20% answered yes

Would you share your mate?

98% answered no (some even used curse words to describe their word NO)

2% answered yes

Have you ever experienced times when you could not achieve an erection?

50% answered yes

50% answered no

If yes, how did you feel?

"Very bad"

"Disappointed"

"Ashamed"

"Angry and hurt"

"It ruined my night"

"I did not want to try it again with the

same woman"

The survey questionnaire contained 90 questions. I've only given responses from 28 of these questions. A questionnaire survey form is included in the appendix. If you would like to complete the survey for your sexual awareness or to mail back to me, feel free to do so.

Chapter 5

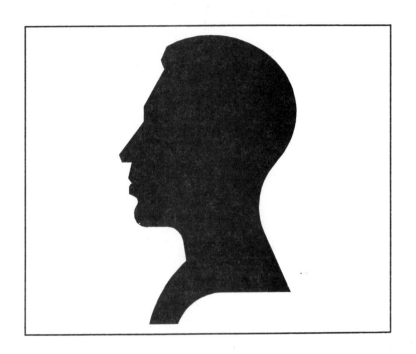

Why the Black Man Fakes Orgasms

Do Black men really fake orgasms? Black men in particular are under great sexual performance pressure. Sex has been viewed as an activity wherein the male is the aggressive partner. The responsibility has been placed upon him to control the outcome of pleasure for himself and his partner.

Yes, they do fake orgasms. Some of the reasons given by men for faking orgasms are some of the same reasons that are given by women. Later in this chapter we will examine responses given by men as to their reason for faking orgasms. According to Bernie Zilbergeld, Ph.D.:

> The traditional model of sex most of us were trained in focuses on male performances. The man has to make the right moves, has to get and keep an erection for as long as necessary, however long that might be, and, now that women are entitled to sexual satisfaction, also has to provide an ecstatic experience for his partner. Just how he's supposed to know what his partner needs and wants are questions for which there are no clear answers. This model puts enormous pressure on the man to perform and leads to unnecessary anxiety and fakery of all sorts (pretending to be interested when he isn't, pretending to have orgasms, women aren't the only ones who do this). For men, the traditional model of sex amounts to playing against a stacked deck. Maybe we need to start stacking the deck on our side.

The following is a excerpt from Dr. Joyce Brother's book:

"Thrusting and panting is easy to fake," I said. "And as for being wet inside, it is not necessarily from the ejaculation. A woman lubricates when she is sexually aroused. And if you use a cream or jelly as part of your birth control, you are even wetter inside. The amount of ejaculation is not all that much, you know a teaspoon or so. Even less."

"But why would a man fake?" Shirley asked. "Men have their problems too," I told her.

"Some kinds of medication can inhibit orgasm. The man can pump away forever and never come. So he fakes. It is a terrible blow to a man's ego to admit that he cannot come."

"Sometimes there is an element of hostility involved. If a man feels resentful about something his wife has done or said, he may fake an orgasm just to get the whole thing over within a hurry."

One man told me that he faked orgasm because he didn't want his girlfriend to know that he could not make it the second time. He pretended to be so excited that he had to come almost immediately.

Medication can inhibit the male orgasm. He can totally exhaust himself and not come. It is a blow to a man's ego not to be able to come. So he will fake it. When a man is angry or resentful toward his partner and really does not want to be bothered, he fakes it. In other words, men fake orgasms for some of the same reasons women do. When a man is preoccupied, his penis can go limp while in the vagina. When he feels that occurring, what do you suspect he is going to do?

More and more secrets about men are now unfolding and they are beginning to fight back. Now that you have gained a better insight as to why men fake orgasms; you should be able to develop a better relationship with your man, wherein faking orgasms will no longer be necessary.

The following are responses from a survey I conducted on male sexuality.

During my research I asked men do they fake orgasms and if so why?

36% answered yes

64% answered no

Some of the reasons given for faking orgasms were:

"I did not have my mind on sex"

"I wanted to get it over with"

"I was tired"

"I did not want her to be disappointed because she could not make me come.

"I get tired of her waiting for me for everything"

"Yes, I fake it a lot when I am under stress at work, that is why I like to masturbate because I can do what I want to without the pressure of someone else to perform."

I do hope that women are not disappointed by discovering that men do fake orgasms.

Chapter 6

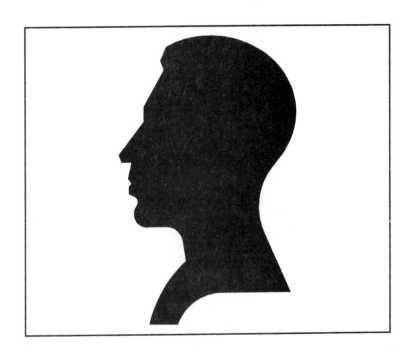

The Black Man's Fears

It is a known fact that all men have fears. Men of all ethnic backgrounds have fears relating to their sexual performance. Many men entering into a sexual encounter are afraid that they may not meet their women's expectations. Women are now more sexually aggressive and feel entitled to sexual satisfaction and demand it. This brings about more anxieties and fears for the Black man because, above all men, he is expected to be good and better in bed.

Many Black men are not permitted to have any involvement with their children following a divorce. In most cases, he is deprived of family contact because he cannot provide financially. This dilemma causes many Black men to have the fear of being isolated from their families.

The Black man who has a good position and a high salaried job also suffers those fears because he understands that he will be among the first in line if a cutback becomes necessary. No matter what status of employment the Black man holds, he is always insecure. He will always be insecure because he is not the one who decides his employment destiny.

The Black man is the only man that is reminded daily via newspapers, magazines, radio and television talk shows of his dismal present and future. Andrew Hacker in his book *Two Nations* had the following to say:

> At the time of this writing, over half a million Black men are in jails or prisons, and as many more could be sent or returned there if they violate their parole or probation. And perhaps as many as a million more have records or are felons, not the best credential for employment. Another large group is debilitated by drugs or alcohol or mental illness.

An article entitled "Status of Black Males" in the December 22, 1993 issue of the *Wave Newspaper* reads as follows:

> On the other hand, and most disturbingly, is a more negative trend. It is a trend...characterized by school failure, unemployment, arrest, criminal record and, indeed then, the inability to generate new Black families that can serve, in a potent way, both the Black community and the State of California. Among the startling statistics raised by the commission after its first two years were: 48% of Los Angeles County's Black males 21 to 24 years old are gang members, versus less than 10% of the White, Latino and Asian county residents.

An article entitled "In California: Future Bleak for Black Men: Worse Than Elsewhere" in the December 30, 1993 issue of the *Los Angeles Sentinel* reads as follows:

> The scenario is neither new nor pretty when it comes to the quality of life of African American males. Cases in point: Black males nationwide on the average live 8 years less than White males; Black males are four times more likely to die from AIDS than White males; homicide rates for Black males are seven times that of White; White males are twice as likely than Blacks to graduate from college or secure stable employment; and Black males are a disproportionate bulk of the U.S. prison population. In California, the status of Black males not only mirrors, but according to state statistics is worse than the national trend.

The same issue of the *Los Angeles Sentinel* was an article written by Evelyn Yoshimura. "A Japanese American Remembers Growing Up In Watts," had the following to say:

> I realize that there are certain things that a Black kid cannot do that other kids take for granted. I remember another time a group of us went up to Hollywood. We were in three separate cars and decided to meet at the Graumann's Chinese Theater. We got separated from the third car. We kept driving back and forth looking for them. Finally we discovered they got pulled over by

the police. It was the car with the only Black guy in our group driving. None of the rest of us got pulled over. Only his car. He wasn't doing anything we weren't. It was then that it really struck me. Blacks have to put up with this all the time. Other people don't really understand this and don't believe it actually happens. But it does, and when you keep getting this message on a day-to-day basis that you are looked at as inferior, it begins to affect you after awhile.

An article in *Business Week* entitled "The Economics of Crime" in the December 13, 1993 issue made the following statements:

Crime is an American tragedy, especially for Blacks. African Americans are disproportionately both perpetrators and victims of criminal violence.

Blacks make up almost half the country's prison admissions, and nearly one in four Black men between the ages of 20 and 29 are in prison, on parole, or on probation. And homicide is the leading cause of death among Black youths. Says Marian Wright Edelman, President of the Children's Defense fund:

"We lose more Black men to guns in our cities in one year than we lost to all the lynchings after the Civil War."

The Black man is the only man that has been blamed for every problem of his race. Women who do understand the Black man's dilemmas can clearly understand the reasons that many Black men appear so strained. These dilemmas are some of the reasons why many Black men have difficulties in areas such as: Male-female bonding, commitment to marriage and commitment to one woman. Many Black men find more emotional comfort in a live-in arrangement versus a marriage relationship.

Haki R. Madhubuti made the following observations:

Too often in the Black community, many of its members, mainly men, don't want to go the legal route to marriage. The legalization of marriage forces partners to struggle with each other at a high level when times are hard. Without a license, brothers and sisters can "walk" at the slightest problem or provocation. Without marriage (that is, some bonding tradition that sanctions and forces "partners" into commitments beyond the bedroom), families would soon die; or other types of families would form.

Fears and anxieties greatly impact sexuality. All a Black man will or will not do in bed or out of bed is a result of his self-image derived from his total life experiences.

Many Black men experience much fear because of their lack of economic empowerment. They are the last to obtain employment, disability benefits, unemployment benefits and mortgage loans. Merely providing the basic needs for his family becomes a constant challenge for the Black man.

Manhood is measured by acquisitions such as power, land ownership and money. Unfortunately most Black men find themselves lacking such acquisitions. A man is expected to provide for and to protect his family, which he has not been allowed to do beginning with slavery. Since the White man is the man that all men are measured by in America: The Black man is made to feel less than a man because he cannot deliver the "American Dream."

The following is a list of fears shared by Black men:

"I fear being dumped by my woman for someone who can offer her more."

"I fear making it financially"

"I fear for my children's safety"

"I fear being killed"

"I fear being jailed for something I did not do and not having the money to fight back"

"I fear getting AIDS"

"I fear getting some woman pregnant whom I may not want for a wife"

It is important that women understand that fears impact the Black man's sexuality. With a clear understanding of these dilemmas, women will be able to embrace the Black man with a deeper love and sensitivity.

Chapter 7

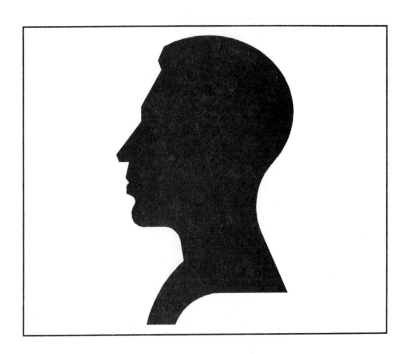

Why Black Men Choose White Women

I want to make it understood that I am not against interracial marriages. Everyone should have the right to choose their own soul mate. This chapter is designed to examine reasons why Black men are choosing White women. According to the U.S. Census Bureau, one out of every 20 marriages are interracial. There were 246,000 Blacks married to Whites in this country last year, almost four times the number in 1970. According to statistics, the number of Black men that are married to White women far out-number any and all other cross-cultural marriages.

Given the facts that approximately 43% of African Americans homes are headed by a female, (according to the U.S. census report) the decrease in the numbers of available African American men, the number of well educated and beautiful African American women, it seems to be about time that we examine the reasons why Black men are increasingly seeking White women.

Why do some Black men choose White women? It is believed that some of the reasons are: The White woman for years has been portrayed as the very essence of beauty and the epitome of all that which is good. She is portrayed in movies, magazines and advertising commercials as a sex symbol. As the viewers view commercial advertisement, the White woman's breast, her nearly nude body and her butt wiggling is supposed to be what sells the beauty and value of the product.

America has done a great job of selling the White woman; hence, it is not just the Black man who feels his self-esteem is heightened by having her. However, this book addresses the Black man.

Many Black men have never witnessed romance between their mother and father. In fact many of them do not see their fathers. Their orientation to hot juicy dripping romance was what they saw in the movies or on T.V. between the White male and the White female. Their normal and natural responses were to lust for such juicy encounters with the White woman.

The Black woman has been portrayed very negatively in the movies. It has been just recently that you have seen her passionately make love in movies. You have seen her being raped, being abused, or offering to perform oral sex for the exchange of drugs. You read about the Black welfare queens, the ones that are on the county, the statistics of those who have babies and are not married, and how many of them will never be married. The Black woman has been given such titles as: gold diggers, sapphires, male bashers and bitch. She has also been labeled as being domineering and sexually inhibited.

Stories are told as to how judges take the Black man to the cleaners during a divorce from a Black woman. It is not widely publicized how much the White woman gets when she divorces the Black man.

Andrew Billingsley, Ph.D. in his book *Climbing Jacob's Ladder* had the following to say:

> The preponderance of African-American men and White women in interracial marriages produced a theoretical explanation of interracial marriages. Developed in 1941 by both Robert Merton and by Kingsley Davis, and supported by Robert Staples, this theory holds that African-American men are attracted to White women because their white caste status elevates the Black partner's sense of importance.

Why else do Black men cross the racial line? Scholars suggest that Black girls may be socialized by their mothers differently than Black boys. I would tend to agree. Black women remember mostly pain associated with White men during slavery. The pain of abuse and raping. Many were raped at the early age of 13 years old. The Black man was raped also by the White woman; however, it provoked no physical pain but psychological damage was done. Many of them enjoyed the sex they had with the White woman because they saw it as a way of getting back at Mr. Charlie for having sex with their wives.

Many Black men were encouraged as boys by their fathers and friends to "get you some White pussy man." I remember hearing men who lived in southern states asking men who had returned from northern states questions such as "man, did you get you some White pussy?"

Black men like any other man want the best that life has to offer and many Black men think that having a White woman is having the best. The best looking (as beauty in American has been measured by European standards). The best sex--as they have heard and seen the White woman's sexual practices in pornographic movies and magazines for years. A pushover (as it has been said that the White woman is very submissive to the Black man). Some believe that the White woman may be more submissive to the Black man because he treats her the way that she has been portrayed, as a precious stone, a royal queen and virgin mary (once she gets out of bed).

An article by Susan Crain Bakos entitled "What Are These Men Afraid Of (Sexually)?" in *New Woman*,

January 1994 magazine stated the following:

> Number one on the average man's sexual wish list is
> more fellatio. They love the physical sensations, the
> complete attention being lavished upon the penis, and
> even the feeling of being erotically under your power.
> Yes, they want more fellatio, but they also want their
> woman to get pleasure from performing it.   You
> probably feel the same way about cunnilingus; you want
> it, but not from a man who is secretly thinking, Oh,
> yuck! as he does it.

I will reiterate that all men share something in common, and the desire for fellatio is one of those things
that men have in common. Oral sex has been viewed as
a cultural thing for Whites. For years they were the only
ones seen doing such in pornography movies and in
pornography magazines.

During my research, I discovered that many Black
men deny oral sex involvement. Don Spears says *In
Search Of GOODPUSSY*:

> There are several reasons why most Black men still deny
> that they perform oral sex on women. The most
> obvious reason is that some Black men really do not do
> it, and they probably never will. One of the reasons
> why those who do continue to say that they do not,

however, is that they see oral sex as a "A White Man's Thing." In fact, they know Black people in general believe anything that it not normal is something that sick White people do.

Another reason for denial is that many Black people tend to be moralistic and any sex act that is not missionary is wrong. Doing it any way but the right way is nasty.

During my survey, many Black men shared with me the following information: "most Black women that performed fellatio did so only to please their men." They stated that they had to request it from the Black woman, whereas with the White woman it was a natural component of making love.

I remember the times when the most degrading and humiliating and inhumane words that Blacks could say to each other were "you suck my pussy or you suck my dick" or to call one a cocksucker. That was like talking about one's mother. Those were fighting words, not love and romance words.

Andrew Billingsley, Ph.D. stated in *Climbing Jacob's Ladder*:

Moreover, these scholars point to the differential bases

on which men and women select their mates. Women give greater weight to such factors as earning capacity and ambition. Men, on the other hand, are more likely to choose their mates on the bases of physical attraction. This suggests that in contemporary American society, White women are more likely to find Black men who meet their potential earning criteria than White men are to find Black women who meet their European conception of physical attractiveness. Conversely, Black men, many of whom have internalized the same European conceptions of physical attractiveness, are more likely to find White women who meet their criteria.

Why do some Black men choose White women? During a recent survey I asked Black men questions regarding their sexual attitudes toward White women. The following is the list of questions and responses:

Have you ever made love to a non-Black woman?

      75% answered no
      25% answered yes

If your answer is no, do you have a desire to do so?

      70% answered no
      30% answered yes

In your opinion is there a difference in bed between the Black woman and the non-Black woman?

"Yes, Black women seem to have the ability to make sex more enjoyable and unforgettable, no matter what the situation"

"Yes, one is Black and the other is White"

"White woman are easier to get and she is more open to do the wild things that men enjoy"

"The Black woman moans and groans, gets you more excited"

"White women are not as quick to show sexual frustration when it ain't right"

Dr. Mack B. Morant had the following to say: "Black men choose White women because they themselves are insane, miseducated, unconscious and self haters." I like the way Dr. Mack B. Morant explains the reasons for the insanity in his book *The Insane Nigger*:

Having complete control over Africa, the colonial powers of Europe projected the images of Africa negatively. They always project Africa in a negative light: jungle savages, cannibals, nothing civilized. Why then naturally it was so negative to you and me, and you and I began to hate it. We didn't want anybody telling us anything about Africa, much less calling us Africans. In hating Africa and in hating Africans, we ended up hating ourselves, without even realizing it. Because you can't hate the roots of a tree, and not hate the tree. You can't hate your origin and not hate yourself. So they very skillfully make you and me hate our African identity, our African characteristics.

You know yourself that we have been a people who hated our characteristics. We hated our heads, the shape of our nose, we wanted one of those long dog-like noses, you know; we hated the color of our skin, hated blood of Africa that was in our veins. And in hating our features and our skin and our blood, why we had to end up hating ourselves. And we hated ourselves. Our color became to us like a prison which we felt was keeping us confined, not letting us go this way or that way. We felt that all of these restrictions were based solely upon our color, and the psychological reaction to that would have to be that as long as we felt imprisoned or chained or trapped by Black skin, Black features and that blood holding us back automatically had to become hateful to us. And it became hateful to us.

It made us feel inferior, it made us feel inadequate, made us feel helpless, and when we feel victims to this feeling of inadequacy or inferiority or helplessness, we turned to somebody else to show us the way.

The above passage gives you a vivid picture of how the Black man was made to hate his African heritage and his physical body. When one hates self, he or she is definitely insane. "When a person hates himself he is insane, his Black woman is an extension of himself; therefore he cannot love her. It is a natural order for a person to want the best things in life. The best thing life has to offer as depicted by the White man is a White woman. He brutally fucked the Black man's woman in the presence of the Black man and his children, diminishing every ounce of pride the Black man held on to. I do not enjoy using profanity; however; I use the word fuck because making love is a sharing and caring experience. He made the Black man believe that the White woman was untouchable, a sacred beauty that no man could venture into except a White man. His "beautiful" White woman was left home only to be admired; while he got his sexual satisfaction from the Black man's woman."

I was told by the elders that when the White men entered a Black man's cabin, the Black man was made to leave the cabin or made to stay and watch. I was told that when the White man finished, he would pat the Black man on the head while leaving and the Black man would say "Massa, I hope you liked it." The White man

126

would respond "yes, good pussy boy" as he went home to his sleeping beauty.

It was common knowledge about the Black women who were the White man's mistress. The relationship of the White men and Black women were the major factors in creating the brain damage the Black man has today for the White woman. When any individual is kept away from something a long period of time by threats, he becomes curious.

Many Black men who fought hard in the Civil Rights Movement were more interested in being able to have the White woman than going to school together, eating together and riding the bus together. The following is an excerpt from Dr. Mack Morant's book:

Eldridge Cleaver in his book, *Soul on Ice,* gives this analysis. There is no love left between a Black man and a Black woman. Take me, for instance. I love White women and hate Black women. It's just in me, so deep that I don't even try to get it out of me any more. I'd jump over ten Nigger bitches just to get a White woman. Ain't no such thing as an ugly White woman. A White woman is beautiful even if she's bald headed and only has one tooth. It's not just the fact that she's got smooth, White skin. I like to lick her White skin as it's sweet, fresh honey flows from her pores, and just to touch her long, soft, silky hair. There's softness about a White woman, something delicate and soft inside her. But a Nigger bitch seems to be full of steel, granite hard and resisting, not soft and submissive like a White woman. Ain't nothing more beautiful than a White woman's hair being blown in the wind. The White woman is more than a woman to me...she's like a goddess, a symbol. My love for her is religious and beyond fulfillment. I worship her. I love a White woman's dirty drawers. Sometimes I think that the way I feel about White woman, I must have gotten from my father and his father's father as far back as you go into slavery.

According to Dr. Mack Morant, Black men who get married to White women are also trying to satisfy socio-psychological insanity in which they suffer in America. For example, this was the response of a Black man from Mississippi when he was asked why he married his White wife.

What did I like best about Carol? That she was hard to get. Her being White had a lot to do with it. The idea I wasn't supposed to have a White woman. After I knew that everyone was going to be against it, I thought, well if I'm successful, I will be the first to do it. But actually it wasn't all that. It's legal now, but I believe I would have done it anyway. It wasn't because

I wanted to make a big bang out of it. I really married her because I loved her. I would say the White woman is much better than the Black woman.

Some of the reasons given by the Black man as to why they date White women are: "When I am with a White woman I feel like a man." (Remember, schemes of White Society has labelled the Black woman as strong and the Black man weak; therefore he feels strong with a White woman). "Also it gives me great pleasure for the White man to see me with his woman, the forbidden fruit."

Another reason for Black men being with White women is that White women are all but molesting Black men. They are pulling after the Black man as though he is the only man left on earth.

The White woman has heard so much about the Black man's sexuality, such as the "Mandingo" "Long John," full of energy, eveready and long endurance. Therefore, she now aggressively seeks him. The man whom she has been denied the opportunity to enjoy like the White man enjoyed the Black woman.

The most critical reason Black men choose White women is because they continue to measure Black women by the European belief and value system. They

129

view the Black woman as an Ebony Caucasian. Black men have not been stimulated nor motivated to dissect the Black women and to examine her unique past and present experiences that causes her behavior and sensitivity to be unique while functioning under the belief and value system that is not her own. The following quote by Victoria King in *Manhandled* expresses the sentiment of the statement:

Of course you will say, "How can I love and want to be with you when I come home and you're looking like a slob? Why White women never open the door for their husbands the way you Black bitches do."

I should guess not, you ignorant man. Why should they be in a such a state when they've got maids like me to do everything for them? There is no screaming at the kids for her, no standing over the hot stove; everything is done for her, and whether her man loves her or not, he provides...do you hear that, Nigger? PROVIDES!

Shahrazad Ali in her book *The Black Man's Guide to Understanding the Black Woman* has the following to say:

The Black woman sees the Black man integrating too. She witnesses him dating and marrying the White woman so she considers her part of the contribution to the 50,000 Black women who date and marry White men as small significance. And others of them complain that the Black man is with the White woman because she is easier to get along with, or that she gives him better sex, or that she respects him more. She doesn't know that he is with her for one reason only , he is with her because she gives him peace.

However it is described, the end result he sees for himself is peace. Of course there are a few who claim they are with the White woman because they are getting back at the White man or that they want to possess her because they were denied her. These are all flimsy and flaky excuses for not being familiar with the word peace. Certainly not all cases are the same.

Earl Ofari Hutchinson, Ph.D. explains the following about Black men and White women:

Ninety-five percent of Black men marry Black women. Most of the guys that marry White women don't do it because they think these woman are Green Goddesses, forbidden fruit or possess mythical status. Nor do they marry them because they are lustful or filled with self-hate. They marry them for the same reason Black men marry Black women. They share common interests, and they love them. Every Black woman worried sick that all Black men want White women should take this test. Think of all the Black men you know. Now how many of them exclusively pursue, date, are married to, or spend every working moment chattering about White women? Don't cheat.

Many reasons have been given as to why Black men choose White women. I have heard and read reasons as simple as opposites attract. The Black man wants to get revenge. It is God's way of bringing all people together. And many more. I suspect that we will find the real answer to the question when Black men become comfortable enough to open up and share the real truths.

Chapter 8

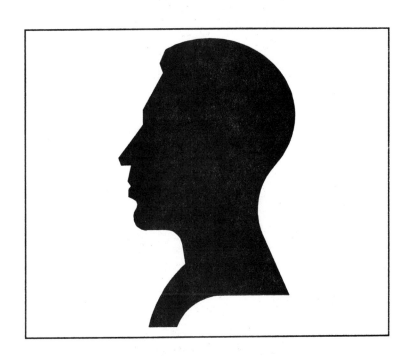

Benefits When Making Love With Men Over Forty

I have interviewed hundreds of men over forty regarding their sexual appetites and sexual performance. During my interviews, men were asked to explain, in detail, any and all changes that they noticed in their sex life upon becoming 40+. Of course, some lied. I believe the men who lied the most were over fifty. You know there are three S's that people generally lie about--sex, size and salary.

One conversational response went something like this: "I am fifty-nine and I feel the same way I did at seventeen. In fact, I wake up with a hard-on more often." I said to him, "yes you just might wake up with a hard-on more often because you have to pee more often." I then said, "you can tell me the truth, I won't tell."

I asked him if he got an erection as quickly as he did during his early twenties. He said, "oh no, it takes more playing around with my penis." He then had to laugh at himself. He said, "I guess I lied a little, huh?" I said to him, "this is a subject that many people are untruthful about." He said to me, "I would think that if you really wanted to know about how men over forty perform sexually, you should ask women who make love to men over forty." I told him that I had asked women also.

He became eager to learn about these women's

responses. After sharing responses with him, he was elated to learn that the changes that come with aging that are perceived as a liability for a man, are viewed as an asset from a woman's point of view.

During my survey, I asked men questions such as:

Do you find that you need more or less stimulation to obtain an erection?

Which area provides you the best and highest stimulation?

Is this the area that provided you the highest and best stimulation during your earlier years?

Do you climax more or less now?

Do you feel the need to ejaculate each time you have intercourse?

Do you explain to your partner that you do not always ejaculate when having sex?

What do you enjoy the most, making love or having sex?

Does your penis get as hard as it did when you were younger?

Are you lasting longer now since your body is not being pressured for quick ejaculation?

Are you now able to obtain a second good erection in a shorter span of time when you do not ejaculate?

I conducted a survey on hundreds of women who are sexually involved with men over forty. I will now discuss some of my findings, discoveries and benefits when making love to men over forty.

First, let me discuss my findings as related to the responses from my survey regarding younger men whom these women had sexual encounters with. I am discussing the young man's sexuality only because I want the reader to gain a sense of the real benefits of making love with men over forty.

Younger Men

Younger men have sex while men 40+ make love.

Younger men obtain an erection quicker and he does not need his woman's help to do so.

Many younger men are impatient when it comes to making sure that their partners are turned on.

Many younger men are eager and ready to ejaculate

right from the start.

Younger men's sexual goal and objective is to ejaculate.

Younger men focus more on their penis and the physical experiences.

40+ Men

He needs more time and more direct penis stimulation to obtain an erection.

He sometimes needs his woman's assistance in helping him to climax.

He understands the value of marinating and flavoring the body before intercourse.

Apart from ejaculation, he enjoys the sexual experience.

Instead of focusing on the hardness of his penis, he focuses on the physical and mental experience.

He does not ejaculate each time with intercourse.

He does not have the need to ejaculate each time (this is normal).

What women enjoy about making love with 40+ men.

Most women want and appreciate more physical stimulation prior to intercourse. The man over forty needs more also; therefore, it becomes a win-win affair for both of them

A woman needs to feel as though she plays a major role in helping her man achieve his firm erection. This gives her a feeling of having sexual power.

Women feel good about their lovemaking skills when they can feel responsible for their men's ecstasy.

The following excerpt is from *Sex Over 40* by Saul H. Rosenthal, M. D.:

"Lovemaking also lasts a lot longer. Young men seem ready to ejaculate from the beginning, but Bob actually needs my help to climax at times. I can usually bring him to climax by making strong, active movements during intercourse. It's really fun watching him as I move. It makes me feel as if I'm giving him his climax, and that makes me feel like a skilled and sexy lover. I also really feel appreciated.

"The whole experience is more tender and sensitive and

sensual and lasts longer. I think that all women like this."

As a younger man, the dominant theme in your sex life was the need to ejaculate. You became erect with little or no direct physical stimulation and were always in a hurry to proceed to intercourse. While you may have felt proud of this ability then, the pressure for rapid intercourse and rapid ejaculation doesn't fit the needs of most women, who usually take a little longer to get sexually excited. They may find younger men impatient, self-centered, and not willing to take the extra time needed to help a woman get aroused as well.

Men over forty get joy from pleasing their women. Men do not feel the need to ejaculate every time with intercourse. Therefore, they can relax themselves and focus on providing pleasure for themselves and their partners. (Not climaxing each time with intercourse for the man over forty is a natural occurrence.)

Making love to men over forty adds a new dimension to lovemaking. Particularly for the couple who understands that ejaculation is just a part of making love. With this understanding, a woman can make love to her man for a longer time and enjoy every inch without feeling inadequate because he does not ejaculate.

Please note, this chapter is not intended to excite younger women to seek older men. I am not saying that younger men are not good lovers. I am saying that older men have had a longer time to practice. One must also understand that "Father Nature" will cause a man to:

"Work smarter instead of harder."

"Slow down and enjoy the scenery during the trip."

"Understand that the sexual race is not determined by the swift or the strong--but by he who holds out to the finishing line."

One last and final big-big-big benefit. The man over forty who did not ejaculate when his woman reached her climax is good for many more rounds. Remember, there is a waiting period between erections for a man after he ejaculates. Because many men over forty do not ejaculate with intercourse each time, you are in a position to enjoy being taken to earthy heaven back-to-back and repeat-repeat. The sports term "Three-Peat" has a new and more enjoyable meaning.

I hope that this chapter will help those women who are in relationships with men over forty. I trust that after reading this book, women will learn to take what they have and to make what they want and learn to stay at home.

Chapter 9

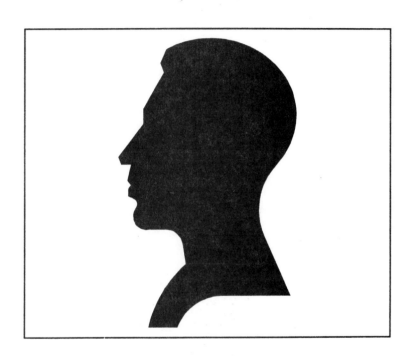

Recipes For Sexual Fulfillment

Satisfying the Black man sexually begins with making him feel special, loved, understood and respected. Contrary to what you have heard, most men want to be pampered. Women must realize that men like to have their mind stroked.

What is sex? Sex is a physical and emotional communion between two people that enhances and deepens love. Men seek sex for pleasure, closeness, reassurance, comfort, release from tension, escape and as a sleeping pill. Sex is good and it is good for you when it is good. After eating, sex is the most sought after drive.

There is a dark side to sex--when it is used to dominate, degrade and to hurt. The Black man does not need to be dominated, degraded nor hurt. He has had more than his share of each. Many Black men only allow themselves to get involved physically when they have sex. Many of them have been so emotionally scared that they mentally construct a wall to shield their emotions.

It takes more effort to bring about an emotional communion between the Black man and his partner. The Black man is always on guard in order to protect himself from hurt and pain. Do not misread me, I am not saying that Black men have not been enjoying sex.

What I am saying is that many of them have only experienced a physical ecstasy. Sexual fulfillment is when a man can experience a physical and emotional ecstasy.

I have had men call me on talk shows expressing their concern regarding being over-sexed as they describe it. Many times after hearing their story, I conclude that they were not over-sexed, but that they were not experiencing an emotional ecstasy. In order for a man to experience sexual fulfillment his <u>mind</u> as well as his <u>behind</u> must be satisfied. The sad reality is that many men have not allowed themselves to experience total ecstasy because of pain, fear and past relationships.

Men who have not experienced sexual fulfillment according to my definition are like women that have not experienced an orgasm. Let me break it on down to the ground: "The ride was good, but it was not the best ride s/he could have had."

I've often wondered why it is that there are classes on every "how to" except how to provide sexual fulfillment for your partner. There is a little information on sexual fulfillment via self masturbation. It seems to be the assumption that providing and receiving sexual fulfillment is a natural occurrence.

Allow me to describe sexual fulfillment as it has been told to me by men. One man stated that "sex is good when it is only physical; however, when one is emotionally charged the feeling is overwhelming. In fact it is a frightening feeling. You feel vulnerable because you sense a loss of control." A man must be careful who he allows to take him to such depth.

He further explained that women think that an erection for the man signifies his readiness for sexual intercourse, he said however that is not the fact. The erected penis is only a physical readiness and women need to get past what they see and try to tap more into their man's emotional status.

A woman should pay attention to a man's body language. She should be aware of his breathing, his firm grip as he holds her, his eyes, his body movement and the sounds he makes as she touches and strokes his body. A woman cannot read a man's penis. He further stated that he makes it a point to avoid an erection in order to get more foreplay from his woman. "After all, women do not recognize the importance of foreplay for their men."

Foreplay. Foreplay is not a woman's thing. Men also enjoy the luxury of foreplay. The excitement created prior to intercourse determines the height and depth of your man's sexual pleasure. Foreplay provides an opportunity for a woman to discover and to explore her man's erogenous zones.

Brigitte Nioche in *What Turns Men On* made the following observation:

> The preparation, and anticipation is at least half the fun of anything we do, but when it comes to lovemaking, foreplay is more than just anticipation. As one man wrote: "How can anyone be a good athlete without exercise?" For that matter, since we are making an analogy to sports here, a warm-up period.
>
> Warming up starts with little things: a look, a teasing glance, a sexual remark, stroking his chest.

For many people, however, the word "foreplay" means sex, whereas, it only implies and leads to making love. And unless you allow yourself and your lover the time to get warmed up, lovemaking is not what it should be. Remember, it's how you get there that makes being there better!

Foreplay for men over forty. Men over forty require more stimulation to the penis for an erection. In other words, men over forty need more foreplay. As Saul H.

Rosenthal, M.D. says in *Sex Over 40*:

> You will need more direct stimulation in order to get erect. One thing you can count on is that when you are over forty you won't be getting spontaneous erections in the same rapid and easy way you did when you were in your adolescence or early twenties. At that age, just the thought of sex, seeing your undressed partner, or a fantasy about a sexual situation would cause your penis to spring to attention in a matter of seconds.
>
> This just isn't going to happen anymore. As you mature, all the physiologic systems in your body slow down--including this one.
>
> It's important to realize that you don't have to wait for an erection to start lovemaking. Your partner can help you get hard and you can make love whenever the two of you desire.

If your man is over forty, his erection may not be as "hard" as it used to be. However, it does not have to be rock hard in order for the both of you to experience the joy of sexual fulfillment.

It is important that a woman understands that a man over forty has less need for climax. According to Masters and Johnson, some men cut down their frequency of lovemaking as they get older because of their decreased desire for ejaculation.

A woman must help her man to understand the lovemaking benefits for herself and for her man apart from climaxes and orgasms.

After play. After play is a good way of demonstrating your affection. According to Brigitte Nioche in *What Turns Men On*.

> The way a woman responds to a man after making love tells him more than any words. Second, it tells the other person that what he just did was very good. "Gently hugging and kissing is a way of saying thank you." Here's a good piece of advice:

> "After the climax, a woman should not get up right away, but keep the man inside her until he is ready to exit. Then she should gently stroke the man and talk softly to him."

The following is a description of an orgasmic experience as told by a male friend. "There is a change in your breathing rate, it increases according to the intensity of your pleasure. The eyes are either closed as one experiences ecstasy or they are opened with an upward fixed stare, or they open and close with the rhythm of your breathing. The body begins to feel light as though floating on air. Thrills begin to run down your spine as you feel the muscles in your butt tighten stiff. The muscles tighten all the way down to your toes. At that moment you are in a heavenly like space. This is the feeling that you wish you could capture and put in a jar for later. When a man has a full-blown orgasm he has flashbacks up to two days later. It is like the after shocks from an earthquake. You can be riding in your car, sitting at your desk, or having a conversation with someone and out of nowhere a warm feeling passes through your body that causes a moment's pause in whatever you are doing. Sometimes it can be embar-rassing because your body actually jerks.

"Following a full-blown orgasm your body becomes rigid and is followed by a state of softness and relaxation. The body experiences an uncontrollable tremble or jerky movement. The body becomes so relaxed and you are in such a calm and quiet space that you want to go to sleep." He then said, "you know, talking about it makes me horny." We both laughed for a minute. I then asked him would he like to use my telephone to call his woman and maybe have a little telephone sex. After all, it is good and safe. He fell to the floor laughing. For a minute, I thought I was going to have to call the para-medic. When he finally came back to normal he said "are you trying to make me a freak or something like that?" I said no, I am just trying to enhance your life. I then explained "telephone sex" to him. The information on telephone sex is an excerpt from my book *Satisfying The Black Woman Sexually Made Simple*.

Telephone Sex. If your woman is long distance, an orgasm is just a phone call away. You can make love to your woman via telephone. Making love via telephone can be a gratifying experience. The phone method allows one to be very creative, uninhibited, and talkative. It really allows one to share experiences that one could not share comfortably in person.

Ask your woman what she is wearing? Then tell her step by step how to take off each piece, (e.g., take off your dress and lay it aside; take off your bra and lay it aside; take off your shoes and stockings; get in the bed and lay on your back). Then ask if she is wearing panties. If yes, say to her: "Sweetheart, lift up your buttocks and slide them off." Remember, the bed is not always the place; therefore, you create the scene according to your need and sexual appetite. You explain explicitly, detailed and erotically everything you are doing to her. Since you cannot see the expressions on your woman's face, tell her that she needs to verbally tell you what she is feeling. You will find yourself doing and saying things that you may not feel comfortable doing or saying in person. If your woman has sexual toys, guide her step by step as to what she is to be doing with them. Ask her to let you know what she feels. If she wants you to do something different than what you are describing to her, in order to give her more pleasure, you are to adhere to her request and verbally tell her erotically what you are doing to her and for her.

If your woman is not long distance, you can still have this experience if you have two phone lines. Simply go into a different room in the house and call her. Or call from work. Just pretend that it is long distance. Making love on the phone can be good and safe.

After I finished the telephone sex instructions, he said: "I am having flashbacks." Then he asked, how do you fix your mouth to talk about sex so freely and explicitly being a woman. I replied, the same way that you fix your mouth to talk about it. That is when he became comfortable with me, the guards went down and he began to tell it all. Then he said, "when I am physically and emotionally involved in sex, it is so good and heavenly that I find myself saying oh Jesus, oh Jesus. I realize that I should not even be mentioning Jesus' name while doing such an act. However, I guess Jesus comes to one's mind when one thinks of anything that is good." He further stated that "sometimes I really feel like saying thank you Jesus for allowing me to be able to feel what I am feeling. I do not take this feeling for granted." He was very serious.

I wish you could have experienced his facial expressions and body language. It was at this point that I began to clearly understand what it meant to a man to be sexually satisfied.

One man said to me that he had heard that the eyes are the window of the soul. He said it is such a pleasurable feeling looking into your woman's eyes while experiencing a sexual communion. There is a look in her eye that lets you know that you have touched her very soul. It is like you begin to exchange energy. You feel her energy flowing through your body and your energy flowing through her body. You have a feeling of oneness.

A woman must realize that all men do not have the same sexual response. There are also differences between Black men in their likes and dislikes about sex, and therefore these things should be communicated between sexual partners. While some Black men may have no sexual limitations or inhibitions, other Black men may find certain requests asked of them by their lovers to be demeaning and degrading.

A Black man's sexual experiences, social setting in which he was reared, physical capabilities, religious background and upbringing, all strongly impact and influence how he genuinely feels about sex, how much he enjoys sex, and his willingness to explore various positions and exotic practices during sex. This is the main reason why the Black man's history was expounded on in the previous chapters, so that you would have a better insight into the present nature of the Black man--as a reflection of his past. To understand the present condition of any sex or race, the past condition or history must be examined and understood. If a Black man has a personal history or family history of rape, certainly he will not enjoy any act that makes him feel helpless, controlled or violated.

It is a good idea for sexual partners to explore each other's body and encourage each other to explore his or her body alone. It should become a joint venture to assure the highest possible sexual gratification for both partners.

If your man suffers sexual hang-ups, then it is your responsibility to help him cross those barriers in order that the two of you can have an enjoyable and healthy relationship.

Many times the touching experience for partners are geared toward producing erotic feelings with sexual intercourse as the objective. A man does not want to have sexual intercourse every time his penis becomes erected. I like the way Adele P. Kennedy and Susan Dean, Ph.D. add flavor to the art of touching in their book *Touching For Pleasure* had the following to say regarding touching:

> Foreplay is usually thought of as a prelude to intercourse frequently becoming only a quick route to total experience of its own, you will have added something of value to your pleasuring repertoire.

Now that you have a greater insight regarding the Black man's sexuality, you should be prepared to give him total sexual satisfaction.

Women must realize that sex does not begin with stroking the body but begins with stroking the mind. Once he has the right mind set, his body will willingly follow. The key is to provide the right atmosphere so that his mind cannot help but be set on loving you totally and completely. Below are a few ingredients that should be added as often as necessary to savor, sweeten, and spice up any relationship by creating an environment and mood more conducive for loving, sex and intimacy.

Be ever mindful as to where he has been and where he is presently.

Be polite and kind.

Remember sex and lovemaking do not start in the bed. They start early in the morning when you pat him on the buttocks or just touch his penis when he is stepping out of bed or when he is leaving the house. (This is like marinating and flavoring a dish you want to cook when you get home.)

Send flowers spontaneously on non-special occasions.

Call him at work just to say, "I love you."

Call to let him know you cannot wait until he gets home.

Have soothing music playing when he comes home.

I discovered during my research that many men have no clue as to what they have been missing from their sexual encounters. After all, you cannot miss what you have never had.

Beginning with his hands is very important in a descending and organized fashion. Begin with his hand, this helps with the anticipation and relaxation process.

Kiss him lightly over the eyelid.

Pull his lip into your mouth softly, gliding your tongue from side to side on his lip.

Seal your lips over his mouth and give a gentle puff of air.

Massage the ear lobes gently in a circular motion.

Glide the tongue over the surface of the ear lobe, softly sucking the ear lobe in between a fixed number of glides. Then, blow small puffs of soothing warm air over the wet surface of each ear lobe.

Give special attention to the nipples. The nipples should be handled with delicacy for good stimulation and excitation. If you are rough with the nipples it will cause pain and pain will cause the muscles to contract. Remember, your sole object is total relaxation.

Now, over the nipples, glide your tongue in a circular motion clockwise then counter clockwise. Then with medium pressure blow warm air over the wet surface of the nipples.

Move to his navel (the belly button). Lightly massage the belly button. Gently massage the pubic area with one hand while the other hand is massaging the nipples of the breast. Massage and kiss the navel. Blow a warm breath of air over the navel. Then begin to stroke the pubic hairs gently while the other hand is massaging the nipples. Move down to his scrotum, the sack that surrounds his testicles. Do not pull upward on the testicles, it will provoke pain. The testicles are very sensitive. Apply massage oil to the scrotum and massage it lightly. He is sure to try to move your hand to his penis right about now. Massage the penis head only for a second.

You are to take control at this very moment, because men tend to be over-anxious to have their erected penis brought to a resolution. It is important to help your man to learn how to relax and to enjoy the full sexual journey. Reassure him that he will regain another erection. The penis is such a sensitive and pleasurable area for the man that he tends to try and rush his woman to it for stimulation and enjoyment.

Do not cause orgasm. If he yells out I am coming, apply the squeeze method technique used for controlling premature ejaculation. The penile squeeze is a very effective method of delaying ejaculation. It is used by almost every sex therapist and has been proven to work. Place your thumb on the frenulum of the penis, with two fingers on the back side, one above the coronal ridge and the other below the coronal ridge. Squeeze tightly and have him tighten his PC muscles. A few seconds before the moment of inevitability. This will inhibit his ejaculatory reflex. Maintain the squeeze for ten to twenty seconds or until the urge to come subsides. Now you may continue the trip that you have started to take him on. You can apply the squeeze or your partner can do it whenever you want to delay orgasm. (See picture illustration in Chapter 4).

Let's move to his feet and then work back to the place where he is dying for you to get back to.

Before massaging the feet, apply a generous amount of oil over the palms of your hands. Start at the tip of the toes and work towards the heel. Pay special attention to his middle toe. According to studies many people report pleasant sexual feelings from rubbing it. This usually relaxes the whole body.

Massage the legs with light strokes proceeding in an upward and downward motion, moving from ankle to knee and from knee to ankle. Massage the thigh lightly with circular and crossing strokes.

Begin kissing and licking his inner thigh. His penis should now be standing at attention again.

When you hit the hot spot you will notice a drastic change in his breathing pattern. Move away from that hot spot and search for other areas to explore. Every now and then return back to that hot spot for another burst of pleasure.

The area near the anus is highly sensitive. Apply pressure and massage the area between the anus and the scrotum. The prostate lies buried inside this area and it is very sensitive to pleasurable sensations.

Pay attention to the breast and chest. Men have the same nerve endings in their chest area as women. There are areas on the body that tends to connect with the penile sensations. When you touch these areas you can feel the sensations in the penis. These areas are the neck, the inner thigh, nipples, chest, middle toe and the area around the anus.

Last, but not least. ***The penis.*** The ridge of the crown and the bottom side of the crown base are said to be the most sensitive parts of the penis. Apply massage oil to your hand and begin an up and down movement on the penis. Massage and stimulate the ridge of the crown and the bottom side of the crown base. Use clockwise and counter clockwise motions using different pressures and speeds. When you see that he will not be able to handle any more then it is time to give him a long good juicy kiss in the mouth and say to your man "tell me when you are ready for me." Tell me how and where. Never assume the bed is the right place. There should be times when you call the shots as related to positions and place. There should be times when your man does the same. Now do what you know is best. Take your man to heaven on earth. Heaven is satisfying a Black man sexually.

As an added "dish" to the recipe for sexual fulfillment, you may consider introducing your man to herbs. For better energy and stamina, consider the herbal approach for your man. Herbs can enhance sexuality for your partners and for you also.

The following is a list of herbs and what they have been used for:

162

Sexual Impotency & Sexual Stimulant
Ginseng
Damiana
Formula I Juice
STIF Herbal Tonic
Chinese Crocodile
Yohimbe

Vitality & Energy
CKLS
Ginseng
Bee Pollen
Formula I Juice

Colon Cleansing
CKLS
Pure Olive Oil
Cascara Sagrada

High Blood Pressure
BP-1
BP-2
Garlic

Prostate
CKLS
Zinc
Uva Ursi
Corn Silk

Weight Loss
Par-K Slim Pack
Chickweed
Bahamian Diet
Chromium Picolinate

Anemia
4-PG
Dandelion

Diabetes
Golden Seal
Capsicum
Chromium
Dia⌂ton

Circulation
Capsicum
Formula I Juice

Brain Booster
CKLS
Gota Kola
Fo Ti Tieng

For more information regarding the herbs, call D&H Market & Health Foods at 213-751-3214.

Conclusion

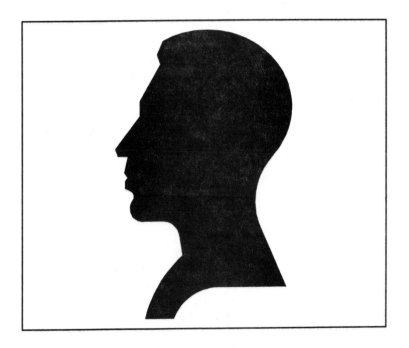

We have travelled a great distance since the beginning of this book. I certainly hope you enjoyed the journey. More importantly, I sincerely hope that you and your partner will benefit from the thoughts shared here, for that was my ultimate goal.

I, like most of us, have seen many relationships destroyed by misunderstandings in the sexual area. This need not be the case. If the techniques and ideas imparted here are adapted to your situation, I am convinced it will make a positive difference. Try it. Simply do s-o-m-e-t-h-i-n-g from this book today, right now if possible. Don't be afraid. If your partner asks where you learned that, show him the book.

And don't feel that you need to copy the ideas verbatim, use them to stimulate your own creative juices. If you think of something new, do it! Remember, two consenting adults can do anything they desire in private. Too often we stifle ourselves. If you do, take action to stop.

Be kind to our Black men whenever possible. They deserve it. They have a dubious distinction in America. If anyone deserves a break, they do. Please don't misunderstand me, everyone should be treated with kindness, you included.

If that has not been the case in your relationship, I suggest you start the ball rolling. Someone has to begin.

I feel like I just heard a collective groan from Black women throughout the United States that sounded like: "Why do *I* have to be the one? Why can't *he* go first for a change?" The answer is simple, if he hasn't in the past, it is highly unlikely that he will in the future without a different motivation.

You can provide that motivation. Few people will take and take and take. If you give more, you will usually get more in return. Try it. You have very little to lose and a lot to gain!!

Good luck and may God bless you.

Appendix

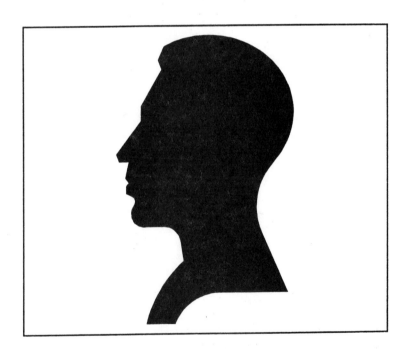

Survey Questions

1.   What is your religious preference?

2.   Are you married? If so, for how long?

3.   Did you complete high school?

4.   Did you complete college? If not, how many years did you attend?

5.   What was your major?

6.   Are you employed?

7.   Are you working in the field of your major?

8.   Where were you born?

9.   Have you ever made love to a non-black woman?

10. If your answer is no, do you have a desire to do so?

11. Why would you make love to a non-black woman?

12. In your opinion is there a difference in bed between the black woman and the non-black woman?

13. How do you feel when you experience premature ejaculation?

14. What do you say to your partner when you experience premature ejaculation?

15. Do you like your partner to express herself verbally during sexual intercourse?

16. What words do you enjoy hearing?

17. Have women ever asked you what turns you on?

18. Have you ever desired more foreplay before sex?

19. Have you ever experienced times when you could not achieve an erection?

   If yes, how did you feel?

20. What are your fears when engaging in sex with a woman to whom you are not married?

21. When your mate is having a sexual affair with another man, do you think it has something to do with what you're doing or not doing?

22. Would you divorce your wife if she was sexually involved with another man?

23.   Would you sever a relationship with your mate if she was seeing another man ?

24.   Would you share your mate?

25.   Do you have any sexual hang-ups?

26.   Name the times, circumstances or happenings when you are not conducive to good sex, (meaning when you cannot put your all into it).

27.   How do you feel when you have had an argument or have been provoked to anger and your mate wants to have sex before resolving the matter?

28.   Do you enjoy oral sex?

29.   Do you enjoy performing oral sex?

      If yes, what do you enjoy about oral sex?

30.   Do you enjoy receiving oral sex from your partner?

      If yes, what do you enjoy about it?

      If no, what are your feelings about people who do?

31. If married, do you feel more comfortable having oral sex with your wife or with an outside woman?

32. Would you marry a woman with whom you have not had sexual intercourse?

33. Are your self-conscious about the size of your penis? (Meaning is your penis too large or too small?)

34. Are you circumcised?

35. What do you expect sexually from a woman?

36. Each time you have sex, do you have an orgasm?

37. Does your sexual partner know when you have an orgasm?

38. Do you fake orgasms?

39. If you fake orgasm, why?

40. What would you like your sexual partner to do when you're experiencing orgasm?

41. Do you masturbate?
    If yes, why?

42. How would you compare an orgasm from masturbation versus sexual intercourse?

43. Do you like to have your penis stimulated by your partner's hands?

44. How do you like your penis stimulated?

45. What part of your penis is more sensuous?

46. What stimulates you the most causing an erection?

47. What activity causes your premature ejaculations?

48. Do you wear condoms?

    If your answer is yes, explain why.
    If your answer is no, explain why.

49. What comes to mind when your partner requests that you wear a condom?

50. Do you enjoy sex less when wearing a condom?.

51. Have you ever told your sexual partner that you were using a condom and you actually were not wearing one?

52. Do you feel that the black man's penis is larger than the white man's penis?

53. Name some myths you have heard about black men?

54. What do you want from your mate in bed?

55. What do you want from your mate out of bed?

56. Name your sensuous spots (hot buttons)

57. Which hot buttons do most women tend to go to?

58. Do you feel just as good having sex with a woman you have just met as you do having sex with a woman with whom you have developed a relationship?

59. What do you tell your son(s) about sex?

60. What do you tell your son(s) about women?

61. Do you feel it is the woman's responsibility to protect herself from pregnancy?

62. Have you ever been in love with two women or more at the same time?

63.   Is it important to you to marry a virgin woman?

64.   Have you ever been treated for any venereal disease?

      If yes, did you tell all the women that you were involved with about it?

65.   Do you like to perform anal sex with your female partner?

      If so, describe the feeling of anal sex versus vaginal sex?

66.   Where is your favorite place you like to have sex? (Meaning bed, floor, chair etc..)

67.   Describe what makes this place more satisfying?

68.   What is your favorite position when having sexual intercourse?

69.   Describe what makes this position more pleasurable?

70.   Is a woman's age an issue for you when looking for a relationship?

71.   Is a woman's age an issue for you when you're looking for sex?

72. Would you teach your son(s) about masturbation?

   If your answer is yes, why?

   If your answer is no, why?

73. Why do men have affairs outside of marriage?

74. If you were to get a woman pregnant outside of marriage, would you marry her?

75. If your son(s) came to you and said "he has gotten a young lady pregnant but, he does not love this person", would you advise your son(s) to marry the young lady?

76. If your teenage daughter came to you and said "she was pregnant...", What advice would you give her?

77. What part of a woman's body turns you on sexually?

78. To satisfy you sexually, does it matter if a woman has small, medium or large breasts?

79. If your partner is under or over weight, would it bother you sexually?

80. Do you fantasize about other women while having sexual intercourse with your mate?

81. What are some of your sexual fantasies?

82. How old were you when you had your first sexual intercourse?

83. How did you learn about sex?

84. Would you date a woman with children?

85. Do you enjoy sex toy(s)?

86. What is your favorite sex toy(s)?

87. How do you feel about dutch dating?

88. How long do you wait to know a woman before you're sexually intimate with her?

89. When you're in bed with a woman, how would you rate yourself sexually from 1-10?

90. Have you ever been sexually bored with your mate in bed?

Bibliography

Aldridge, Delores P. *Focusing Black Male-Female Relationships*. Chicago: Third World Press, 1991.

Ali, Shahrazad. *The Blackman's Guide to Understanding The Blackwoman*. Philadelphia: Civilized Publication, 1990.

Bakos, Susan Crain. "What Are These Men Afraid Of (Sexually)?" *New Woman Magazine* January 1994.

Barashango, Ishakamus. *Afrikan Woman The Original Guardian Angel*. Silver Springs, Maryland: Dynasty Publishing Co., 1990.

Billingsley, Ph.D., Andrew. *Climbing Jacob's Ladder: The Enduring Legacy of African American Families* New York: Simon & Schuster, 1992.

Brothers, Dr. Joyce. *What Every Woman Should Know About Men*. New York: Ballantine Books, 1983.

Dubonsky, M.D., Steven L. "When Sexual Dysfunction, Masks Anxiety and Depression." *Medical Aspects of Human Sexuality* October 1991.

Ende, M.D., Jack. "Screen For Sexual Dysfunction." *Medical Aspects of Human Sexuality*. February 1989.

Hacker, Andrew. *Two Nations Black and White, Separate, Hostile, Unequal.* New York: Charles Scribner's Sons, 1992.

Halbert, Janet. "Start A Low-Fat-Low Cholesterol Diet Now To Prevent Impotency." *The Natural Healing Newsletter*, September 1993.

Hutchinson, Ph.D., Earl Ofari. *The Assassination of The Black Male Images.* Los Angeles: Middle Passage Press, 1994.

Jacoby, Susan. "When Women Lie About Sex." *New Woman Magazine*, December 1991.

Kennedy, Adele P. and Susan Dean Ph.D. *Touching For Pleasure.* Chatsworth, California: Chatsworth Press, 1986.

King, Victoria. *Manhandled.* Memphis: Derek Winston, 1992.

Madhubuti, Haki R. *Black Men Obsolete, Single, Dangerous?* Chicago: Third World Press, 1990.

Martin, Nicholas. "All Hands On Dick." Magazine Unknown

McQueen, William. *The X-Rated Sex Book.* Lake Hiawatha: Margrevar, Inc., 1992.

Milligan, Ph.D., Rosie. *Satisfying The Black Woman Sexually Made Simple.* Los Angeles: Professional Business Consultants, 1990.

Morant, Dr. Mack. *The Insane Nigger.* Holly Hill: R & M Publishing Co., 1978.

Nelson, M.D., John E. "Counseling The Female Partner of A Man With Psychogenic Impotence." *Medical Aspects of Human Sexuality.* September 1987.

Nioche, Brigitte. *What Turns Men On.* New York: Penguin Group, 1989.

Ogden Ph.D., Gina. *Sexual Recovery: Every Woman's Guide Through Sexual Co-Dependency.* Deerfield Beach, Florida Health Communications, Inc. 1990.

Rosenthal, M.D., Saul H. *Sex Over 40.* New York: The Putnam Publishing Group, 1987.

Schwartz, Bob. *The One Hour Orgasm.* Houston: Breakthru Publishing, 1988.

Shaw, M.PR, Valerie B. *Himpressions: The Black Women's Guide To Pampering The Black Man A Manual.* Hollywood: Turn The Page Productions, 1993.

Spears, Don. *In Search of GOODPUSSY: Living Without Love The Real Truth About Men and Their Relationships.* New Orleans: Don Spears, 1992.

Welsing, Dr. Frances Cress. *The Isis Paper.* Chicago: Third World Press, 1989.

Westheimer, Dr. Ruth K. and Dr. Louis Lieberman. *Dr. Ruth's Guide to Erotic and Sensuous Pleasures.* New York: S.P.I. Books, 1992.

Young, M.D., Clinton W. and Daniel W. Lodarazyk, M.D., "Counseling the Impotent Man With Diabetes." *Medical Aspects of Human Sexuality.* March 1986.

Zilbergeld, Ph.D., Bernie. *The Truth About Men, Sex, and Pleasure, The New Male Sexuality.* New York: Bantam Books, 1993.

"The Economics of Crime." *Business Week.* 13 December 1993.

"Status of Black Males." *Wave Newspaper.* 22 December 1993.

BOOKS AVAILABLE THROUGH
Professional Business Consultants
by Dr. Rosie Milligan

Satisfying the Blackwoman Sexually Made Simple - $20.00

Satisfying the Blackman Sexually Made Simple -$14.95

Negroes-Colored People-Blacks-African-Americans in America- $13.95

Starting A Business Made Simple - $20.00

Getting Out of Debt Made Simple - $20.00

--Order Form--------------------------------

Mail Check or Money Order to: 1425 W. Manchester, Suite B, Los Angeles, CA 90047

Name_____Date_____
Address_____
City_____ State _____ Zip Code _____
Day Telephone _____
Eve Telephone _____
Name of book(s) _____
Sub Total $_____
Sales Tax (CA Add 8.25%) $_____
Shipping & Handling $3.00 $_____
Total Amount Due $_____
□ Check   □ Money Order
□ Visa   □ Master Card   Ex. Date _____

Credit Card No. _____
Driver's License No._____

_____   _____
Signature   Date

NOTES

NOTES

NOTES

NOTES

NOTES

NOTES